Hobart Paperback No. 11

KEYNES VERSUS THE 'KEYNESIANS' . . .?

Keynes versus the 'Keynesians'...?

AN ESSAY IN THE THINKING OF J. M. KEYNES
AND THE ACCURACY OF ITS INTERPRETATION BY HIS FOLLOWERS

T. W. Hutchison

Professor of Economics, University of Birmingham

Second Impression

Published by
THE INSTITUTE OF ECONOMIC AFFAIRS
1977

First published in July 1977
Second Impression February 1978
© The Institute of Economic Affairs 1977

ISSN 0309-1783
ISBN 0-255 36101-7

Printed in Great Britain by
GORON PRO-PRINT CO LTD,
CHURCHILL INDUSTRIAL ESTATE, LANCING, WEST SUSSEX
Set in 'Monotype' Bembo

Contents

Preface

The *Hobart Paperbacks* were devised as a series of studies of medium length between *Papers* and books in which economists would analyse the relationship between economic thinking and policy, and in particular consider the circumstances which encourage or inhibit the transformation of one into the other.

The first in the series, the 'theme' volume, was written in 1971 by Professor W. H. Hutt, under the title *Politically Impossible . . .?*. Subsequent numbers have analysed the early economic policies of the 1970-74 Government (Samuel Brittan), the apparent conflict between the intention of the Treaty of Rome and the performance of the commissariat in Brussels (Russell Lewis), the Austrian neo-classical thinking of Professor F. A. Hayek from 1931 to 1972, the economics of bureaucracy (Professor W. A. Niskanen), the Cambridge School of economics (Professor Mark Blaug), recent British economic management (Ralph Harris and Brendon Sewill), and the theory and practice of collective bargaining (Professor Hutt), the theory of public choice and the extent to which economic policy cannot be understood without allowing for the political motivations of government and the occupational interests of its executives (Professor Gordon Tullock and Dr Morris Perlman). The tenth, which reviewed the analyses of IEA authors since 1957 under the title *Not from benevolence . . .*, was a special number on the history of the Institute by the General and Editorial Directors. The present in the series continues the theme of the impact of economic ideas on policy and the influence of economists on the thinking of government and politicians.

It would be common ground among economists of all schools and politicians in many countries that the economist who exerted more influence than any other on world economic thinking and public policy in the last 40 years was John Maynard Keynes. He lived only 10 years after his *General Theory of Employment, Interest and Money*, published in 1936, but his impact on minds and action

ix

has continued almost undiminished until at least the last few years. What Keynes said, or meant, is still disputed, and he is quoted in support by economists and politicians who differ among themselves.

Not least, Keynesian thinking is still closely followed by the Treasury in its advice to Ministers and by the National Institute of Economic and Social Research, the largely government-financed organisation whose generally supposed second opinions seem to be based on different subjective judgements but essentially similar short-run forecasting techniques. Economic advisers drawn from the universities have also, until recently, reflected Keynesian thinking, and one of them, Mr Michael Stewart, has recently defended it as correct but thwarted by the electoral tactics of political parties in reversing their predecessor's policies,[1] as in income and price control.

In this *Hobart Paperback* Professor T. W. Hutchison, author of several works on the history of economic thought, tests the interpretations of Keynes in the light of his writings and utterances within a few years of 1936. He defends Keynes both against several critics and then against former colleagues and students at the University of Cambridge who claim to be, or who are regarded as, Keynesians in their interpretations, development and applications of his system of thought.

Professor Hutchison argues that Keynes would not have supported their interpretations of five major aspects of economic policy: the nature of full employment, the methods of ensuring economic growth, the relative importance of price stability and other economic aims such as full employment, the control of inflation by incomes policies, and the desirability of public expenditure. And from this view he maintains that Keynes's name and repute have been used to support policies not justified by his writings. To indicate the reaction of Cambridge economists, leading exponents of Keynesian economics were invited to comment on Professor Hutchison's text. Lord Kahn and Professor Sir Austin Robinson responded, and Professor Hutchison was given the right of reply.

The reader of this short *Hobart Paperback* will find in it an intriguing assembly of extracts from Keynesian writings and of the interpretations placed on them by economists who have exerted a

---

[1] *The Jekyll & Hyde Years: Politics & Economic Policy since 1964,* J. M. Dent, 1977.

continuing and substantial influence on British economic thought and policy for three decades. Keynesian thinking has come under increasing criticism in recent years, and it has been argued by Professor Axel Leijonhufvud that there is a difference between Keynesian economics and the economics of Keynes.[1] The five issues listed above and others are central to the discussion and formation of economic policy in 1977, over 30 years after Keynes's death, and will continue to be so for years to come. If anyone doubted Keynes's celebrated dictum about the influence of ideas on thought and policy,[2] his work and life are testimony to its strength. No doubt economists will debate for many years what Keynes said, and what he meant. This *Hobart Paperback* is intended as a contribution to that debate.

We have the sad duty of recording our gratitude to the late Professor Harry Johnson who read Professor Hutchison's text and offered comments which embodied possibly his last economic judgement before his final illness in February. The Institute hopes to find a more lasting memorial by which to express its gratitude for Harry Johnson's services to it since he was made an Adviser in 1974 and for his advice on several texts. We should also like to thank Professors Milton Friedman and F. A. Hayek for reading Professor Hutchison's text and for their comments on it.

We have to thank the Editor of *The Times*, and Lord Kahn, Lord Keynes's literary executor, for permission to reproduce the 1937 articles in *The Times* (Appendices A and B).

The Institute's constitution requires it to dissociate its Trustees, Directors and Advisers from the arguments and conclusions of its authors but it presents, for teachers and students of economics, Professor Hutchison's study and the Comments by Lord Kahn and Sir Austin Robinson as an analysis of the views of the most influential British applied political economist in the 20th century so far. Since the exchange also sheds light not only on what Keynes said but also on what he meant, it is of interest to students of the history of economic thought. Not least, since Keynes's influence on economic policy has continued long after his life, the text is perhaps of even

---

[1] *On Keynesian Economics and the Economics of Keynes*, Oxford University Press, 1968; a shortened version is in *Keynes and the Classics*, Occasional Paper 30, IEA, 1969 (6th impression 1977).

[2] Quoted by Professor Hutchison, p. 35, fn. 1.

more immediate interest to British employers and employees, taxpayers and tax-spenders, voters and politicians, consumers and producers, public men and interpreters of economic thought in the press and television.

June 1977   ARTHUR SELDON

The Author

TERENCE W. HUTCHISON, Professor of Economics at the University of Birmingham since 1956, was born in 1912 and educated at Tonbridge School and Cambridge University. Before the war he taught in Bonn and Baghdad, and served in the Indian Army Intelligence, 1941-46, attached to the Government of India 1945-46.

He was a Lecturer (1947-51) and Reader (1951-56) at the London School of Economics, Visiting Professor at Columbia University 1954-55, Visiting Fellow at University of Saarbrücken 1962, Visiting Professor at Yale University 1963-64, Visiting Fellow at Australian National University, Canberra, 1967, and Visiting Professor at Dalhousie University, Halifax, Nova Scotia, 1970, Keio University, Tokyo 1973, and University of Western Australia, 1975. Author of *The Significance and Basic Postulates of Economic Theory* (1938); *A Review of Economic Doctrines (1870-1920)* (1953); *Positive Economics and Policy Objectives* (1964); *Economics and Economic Policy in Britain 1946-1966* (1968); *Knowledge and Ignorance in Economics* (1977); *Revolution and Progress in Economic Knowledge* (Cambridge University Press, forthcoming). For the IEA he has written *Markets and the Franchise* (Occasional Paper 10, 1966) and *Half a Century of Hobarts* (Hobart Paper Special, 1970).

I. Decline and Crisis

Three different sources of weakness and inadequacy may be distinguished in the process of decline and crisis of a once successful, or 'orthodox', system of theory, 'paradigm', or 'research programme' in economics, such as that of English Classical Political Economy or 'the Ricardo-Mill economics', as Jevons called it, or, a hundred years later, Keynesian economics.

1. *Internal crisis*

First, there may be discovered original 'internal', logical or empirical weaknesses, of the kind which arise in the natural sciences, which may accumulate to create a 'crisis'. Keynesian economics, over the last four decades, has undergone interminable examinations and re-examinations in these terms which we do not resume here.

2. *Historical and institutional change*

Secondly, in economics and the social sciences, a very important source, often cumulative, of weakness and inadequacy (unlike, usually, in the natural sciences) consists of changes in historical conditions and institutions. Such changes both give rise to new weaknesses and inadequacies and magnify old ones, by creating empirical anomalies or irrelevances in once more acceptable 'orthodox' doctrines.

In the roughly half-century before the 1860s, for example, institutional and historical changes had rendered the basic theoretical and policy concept of the 'natural wage' much more obviously invalid or inadequate – that is, *either* empirically false, *or* empty. The natural-wage proposition had always been at least questionable, but it remained absolutely central to the theoretical and policy doctrines of 'the Ricardo-Mill economics'. Furthermore, institutional changes had rendered more serious the inadequacies of the orthodox treatment, or non-treatment, of such increasingly important questions as relative wages and the pricing of public utilities and monopolies. Keynesian economics has also been subject to this source, or type, of historical-institutional obsolescence.

3. *Degeneration from doctrine to dogma*

But the degeneration of systems, 'paradigms', or 'research programmes' in economic theory and political economy (and the rise of 'counter-revolutionary' ideas, or 'antitheses') may have a *third* kind of source: the way in which they come to be adapted or altered by disciples, successors, or popularisers. As Professor Martin Bronfenbrenner has explained:

> 'With the passing of the generations, a thesis hardens from doctrine to dogma. Its choirs of angels become choirs of parrots, chanting "supply and demand", "full employment", or "planned society", as the case may be. . . . At the same time, . . . there is leached out of the original thesis whatever implications seem threatening to the ruling class. . . . Because the thesis turns apologetic, repetitive, and lifeless, and also because problems arise for which the answers stemming from orthodox paradigms are either lacking or unacceptable, there develop antitheses to every thesis.'[1]

As regards the 'hardening into dogma', the over-confidence and pretentiousness generated by the initial 'revolution' may be reinforced by short-run, and/or apparent, or superficial, success in policy. That nothing fails like success is liable to be true also in the history of economic thought. For when, and insofar as, the original doctrines are hardened over-confidently into dogmas and protected against testing and re-testing, the flexibility and sensitivity to changing real-world conditions which contributed to the success of the work of the original 'revolutionary' leader may be lost by the epigoni.

Furthermore, the attitude of regarding economic theories – including especially a new 'revolutionary' theory – as on a par, epistemologically, with the theories of the natural sciences (and Keynes was compared with Einstein) may encourage a more exaggerated belief than is justified in the relative durability, and resistance to obsolescence, of the new economic theory or discovery. A more serious development may be that the hardening into dogma and

---

[1] 'The "Structure of Revolutions" in Economic Thought', *History of Political Economy*, vol. 3, 1971, p. 139.

mystique of the original doctrines may bring significant alterations, in emphasis or content, as qualifications and exceptions are forgotten or modified.

This third type, or source, of degeneration may, of course, be combined with the second historical-institutional source. To some extent, for example, both these kinds of process were present during the decline and fall of classical political economy, in which the exaggerations and dogmatisms of over-simplifiers and popularisers played a significant part in rendering the orthodox doctrines more open to attack. During the critical period of the 1860s, for example, such figures as Fawcett and Lowe might be mentioned.[1] It may be still more serious if the epigoni bend the doctrines of the original 'revolutionary' leader in favour of their own policy predilections, or in favour of political forces or trends on whose wave, or 'bandwagon', they may wish to advance. The central theme of this essay relates mainly to this third source of weakness, or process of decline.

---

[1] The fairly sudden decline and fall of English classical political economy, and the nature and processes of 'revolutions' in the history of economic thought, are discussed in T. W. Hutchison, *On Revolutions and Progress in Economic Knowledge,* C U P (forthcoming).

II. Were Keynes's Doctrines Wrong from the Start?

Our main concern is with the wide divergencies between the policy-objectives which Keynes formulated in the last decade of his life, and those propagated in his name in the decades after his death.

Before passing to this main theme we touch, all too briefly, upon the peripherally related question, recently raised, that because 'Keynesian' policies had, in their country of origin, run into obviously very serious difficulties by the 1970s, *therefore* Keynes's own doctrines were fundamentally and fatally flawed from the start. Certainly, by the 1970s it could hardly have failed to escape the attention of open-minded observers that, as Mr Walter Eltis has remarked:

> 'Inflation has accelerated throughout the world, and it must be particularly disturbing to Keynesian policy-makers that the countries where their influence was greatest are those which have suffered most. . . . So how is it, a sensible Keynesian might ask, that the countries where those in power and influence have the most correct understanding of how economies work managed to achieve the worst results and to be among the world's perpetual candidates for international financial support? Ironically, most of this [support] has to come from countries which are managed in non-Keynesian ways.'[1]

Keynes's main doctrines: fatally flawed or irrelevant?

There is obviously a justifiable and searching question here. However, more fundamental criticisms have been expressed to the effect that Keynes's main doctrines were, in their origins, fundamentally invalid or unnecessary, and that their influence, and the whole phenomenon of 'the Keynesian revolution', was irrelevant or even disastrous. Professor F. A. Hayek, for example, has (1975) referred to

---

[1] 'The Failure of the Keynesian Conventional Wisdom', *Lloyds Bank Review*, October 1976, p. 1.

'. . . *the fatal idea* that unemployment is predominantly due to an insufficiency of aggregate demand . . .'[1]

Professor H. G. Johnson, on rather different lines, has argued that Keynes's main doctrines were quite misconceived for dealing with a problem which amounted simply or largely to the over-valuation of sterling between 1925 and 1931:

> 'Had the exchange value of the pound been fixed realistically in the 1920s – a prescription fully in accord with orthodox economic theory – there would have been no need for mass unemployment, hence no need for a revolutionary new theory to explain it . . .'[2]

Five grounds for disagreement with the critics

While fully conceding the force of Mr Eltis's question regarding the difficulties which 'Keynesian' policies had run into by the 1970s, we do not agree with the views of Professors Hayek and Johnson that Keynes's doctrines were fatally erroneous or irrelevant *from the start*. Obviously the passages quoted raise much larger and more complex questions than can be dealt with here. But, very briefly and summarily, there are five main grounds for disagreeing with their fundamental and comprehensive dismissal of Keynes's original doctrines:

1. It seems to amount to a considerable misconception of the order of magnitude of the crisis of depression and unemployment during the inter-war years to suggest that it could all have been avoided by fixing the gold parity of the pound rather differently between 1925 and 1931. The outcome from a lower parity would in any event have depended on the conduct of the money supply. Also, incidentally, the abandonment of the pre-war gold parity would have represented, as Pigou warned at the time, a crucial step – inevitable perhaps in the long run – towards the political control of money, which has indeed followed the later abandonment of gold. Anyhow, the most powerful monetary orthodoxy at the time was in terms of the unchanging *gold* parity of the pound. While leading the attack on it, Keynes showed a reluctant respect

---

[1] *Full Employment at Any Price?*, Occasional Paper 45, IEA, 1975, p. 19 (italics added).

[2] 'Keynes and British Economics', in Milo Keynes (ed.), *Essays on John Maynard Keynes*, C U P, 1975, p. 110; also *History of Political Economy*, Duke University Press, North Carolina, Fall 1974, p. 273.

for the psychological power, in terms of 'confidence', of this long-entrenched orthodoxy, by his refusal to support an abandonment of the gold parity before the final crisis of 1931. It would seem, also, that modern 'monetarist' prescriptions might have run into serious conflicts with the gold-standard orthodoxy.

II. Professor Hayek, in the early 1930s, thought that deflation could restore 'the functioning of the system'. Forty years later (1975) he thought differently:

'I then believed that a short process of deflation might break the rigidity of money wages. . . . I no longer believe it is in practice possible to achieve it in this manner.'[1]

By 1939 Professor Hayek agreed also that:

'There may be desperate situations in which it may indeed be necessary to increase employment at all costs, even if it be only for a short period . . .'[2]

He admitted that Germany under Brüning in 1932 may have been such a case. But in Britain in 1932, with unemployment at over 22 per cent, Professor Hayek opposed a proposal for increased public spending put forward by Keynes, Pigou and others. We would maintain that, in the circumstances of 1932, Keynes and Pigou were right and that Professor Hayek and his colleagues from the London School of Economics were wrong.[3] Professor Hayek's main policy maxim at that time was to keep the quantity of money constant, with the price level falling if the economy was growing. His main and repeated warning was of the dangers of an increase in the quantity of money. He never seemed to refer to the dangers of a contraction or to have envisaged such dangers as currently serious.[4]

III. Unemployment in Britain, between 1921 and 1939, seems almost continuously to have been above anything describable as the natural level, as it may well also have been periodically during

---

[1] *Full Employment at Any Price? op. cit.,* p. 26. It does not seem that Professor Hayek's policy in 1932 would have done anything to counteract what Professor Friedman calls 'the Great Contraction', and might well have worsened it.

[2] *Profits, Interest and Investment,* Routledge & Kegan Paul, 1939, p. 63n, quoted in *Choice in Currency,* Occasional Paper 48, IEA, 1976, p. 11.

[3] *The Times,* 17 and 19 October, 1932, and T. W. Hutchison, *Economics and Economic Policy in Britain, 1946-1966,* Allen & Unwin, 1968, p. 21.

[4] *Prices and Production,* Routledge, 2nd edn., 1935, Lecture 4, on ' "Elastic" Currency'·

the depressions of the pre-1914 business cycle. Unemployment was widely regarded as an increasingly serious problem in Britain well before the First World War. In the inter-war years economic instability and unemployment were leading, outside Britain, to profound social upheavals. It was unemployment between 1930 and 1933 that was to a large extent responsible for bringing Hitler to power, and hence for the Second World War.

IV. There was in Britain no effective alternative to the Keynesian policy proposals in the inter-war years. Indeed, Keynes's proposals were supported by a considerable majority of leading economists, *including Pigou and Robertson.* It would be misleading, and a very unjust reflection on the creative originality of Professor Milton Friedman, to suggest that there was some effective, operational 'monetarist' doctrine, or 'orthodoxy', equipped with adequate statistical material, to combat the over-riding problem of unemployment in the inter-war years. (One is reminded of the great Groucho's indignant exclamation in *Go West* when someone suggested he telephone an urgent message: 'Telephone? This is 1870. Don Ameche hasn't invented the telephone yet.')

Moreover, the predictions in 1929 of the leading quantity theorist and forerunner of 'monetarism', Irving Fisher, do not suggest that any effective, operational alternative then existed in that direction.[1] Keynes's policy-doctrines were not without weaknesses and dangers, but in a profoundly and acutely critical

[1] As evidence we may cite, for example, Fisher's famous pronouncement (15 October, 1929) that 'stock prices have reached what looks like a permanently high plateau ... I expect to see the stock market a good deal higher than it is to-day within a few months'. (Quoted by J. K. Galbraith in *The Great Crash 1929*, Pelican Books, 1961, pp. 95 and 116.) Professor Friedman and Anna Schwartz write on the American literature at this time: 'Contemporary economic comment was hardly distinguished by the correctness or profundity of understanding of the economic forces at work. . . . Many professional economists as well as others viewed the depression as a desirable and necessary economic development required to eliminate inefficiency and weakness, took for granted that the appropriate cure was belt-tightening by both private individuals and the government, and interpreted monetary changes as an incidental result rather than a contributing cause . . . One can read through the annual *Proceedings* of the American Economic Association or the Academy of Political Science and find only an occasional sign that the academic world even knew about the unprecedented banking collapse in process, let alone that it understood the cause and remedy.' (*The Great Contraction 1929-1933*, Princeton University Press, NJ, 1965, pp. 113-5.) Professor Friedman and Anna Schwartz are disregarding the considerable body of opinion which supported proposals of a Keynesian type for countering 'the Great Contraction'. (H. Stein, *The Fiscal Revolution in America*, University of Chicago Press, 1969, especially chapters 1-7.)

world economic situation they were the best, and almost the only coherent, proposals in Britain at the time.

v. Anyhow, the Keynesian 'revolution' was followed after 1945 by what Professor Hayek describes as

'. . . a unique 25-year period of great prosperity . . . [which lasted] for a much longer time than I should have thought possible.'[1]

This is quite a long success, and one cannot help wondering why, since this great prosperity – whether or not it owed anything or much to Keynes's teachings – survived for so long, more caution and moderation could not have kept it going still longer. For, as we shall see, a most influential group of self-styled 'Keynesian' economists was constantly expressing and encouraging discontent with levels of employment in the 1950s and 1960s. Perhaps, in the long run, social and political forces were bound to take over and destroy this prosperity. Indeed, according to Professor Hayek's later views, nothing less than fundamental constitutional restraints on the power of democratic majorities, and the removal from political authorities of any power or influence over the money supply, could prove effective bulwarks against inflation. These views may well seem to possess some valid basis in the 1970s. But it seems difficult to blame Keynes for not taking such a very fundamental, political line in the 1930s, since Professor Hayek himself, apparently no longer believing in the efficacy of the policies he was proposing in the 1930s, only took to this fundamental line some 20 or 30 years after Keynes's death.

Hindsight and liability to obsolescence

With the benefit of hindsight, inadequacies and dangers can certainly be discerned in Keynes's doctrines (as, indeed they were at the time by Pigou, Robertson and Henderson). A more cautious and modest view on the part of his followers on the gains achieved by the Keynesian 'revolution', especially in terms of generality, might have been in order. The dependence of Keynes's doctrines on the special conditions of the time should have received much more emphasis, as should the liability to rapid obsolescence, from which most economic doctrines are liable to suffer. Basically the

---

[1] *Full Employment at Any Price?*, op. cit., p. 15.

most serious weakness was political: that is, an over-optimism, perhaps even naïveté, regarding the possibility of enlightened management of the economy by popularly-elected governments.[1] From time to time, throughout his career, Keynes would castigate politicians in the most scathing terms. But he always rapidly recovered his optimistic belief that, under his tutelage, governments would muster a sufficiency of enlightened altruism to implement his latest proposals for economic management.[2] Nevertheless, in spite of this fundamental political question-mark, we do not accept that because by the 1970s so-called 'Keynesian' doctrines in Britain had run into a 'crisis', or at least into profoundly serious difficulties, *therefore* Keynes's own proposals were originally fundamentally unjustifiable and invalid. For two crucial allowances, or adjustments, have to be made in respect of:

(1) historical changes in conditions and institutions, as compared with those which confronted Keynes; and

(2) the serious alterations made in 'Keynesian' doctrines since his death.

This latter process is what we are centrally concerned with here.

In any event, before a judgement on this issue can be finally passed, what Keynes himself proposed in the last 10 years of his life must be disinterred and stripped of the distorting accretions of myth and propaganda behind which it has become concealed in the decades since his death.

---

[1] R. Skidelsky, 'The Political Meaning of the Keynesian Revolution', *Spectator*, 7 August, 1976, p. 9. [A systematic critique of Keynes's economic policies in terms of the newer theory of public choice in the American context, is mounted by J. M. Buchanan and R. E. Wagner in *Democracy in Deficit*, Academic Press, New York and London, 1977. A British version of the argument will be published in 1978. – ED.]

[2] T. W. Hutchison, 'The Collected Writings of J. M. Keynes, vols. I-VI and XV-XVI', *Economic History Review*, February 1973, p. 142.

III. On How to Avoid a Slump

Most of Keynes's writings on domestic economic policies and policy-objectives were, of course, concerned with conditions extremely different from those in Britain in the 1950s and 1960s. Nevertheless, in various writings in the last 10 years of his life, following the publication of *The General Theory*, Keynes gave strong indications of his views on peace-time policies on employment targets and the avoidance of inflation, which contrast widely with those which became associated with his name in the 'fifties and 'sixties.

Let us begin with some articles written in 1937, one year after *The General Theory* (but not yet made available in his *Collected Writings*).[1] 1937 was a peak year, and unemployment was back around 12 per cent. These articles are probably Keynes's only, or much his most significant, contribution regarding current policies for dealing with the upper turning-point of the cycle, as contrasted with the depths of the depression. Moreover they were his last pronouncements on current domestic policy-problems under peace-time assumptions and it is very remarkable that they have not received more attention. The first of them was entitled 'How to Avoid a Slump'.[2]

Policy proposals to avoid another slump: 'a rightly distributed demand'
Keynes begins by remarking that we have 'climbed out of the slump'. There was not 'a precarious boom'. There was 'nothing wrong', but the time had come to level off activity and above all to take precautions against a descent into another slump. Keynes maintained:

---

[1] I discussed these articles in the Appendix to *Economics and Economic Policy* . . ., *op. cit.*, pp. 295-8, which contains most of the passages from Keynes's letters and articles quoted here. [The articles themselves are reproduced by kind permission of the Editor of *The Times* in Appendix A, pp. 65-73. – ED.]

[2] *The Times*, 12 January, 1937.

'We are in more need today of a rightly distributed demand than of greater aggregate demand.'[1]

He insisted that economists were

'faced with a scientific problem which we have never tried to solve before'.

He claimed – emphasising broad agreement on policy questions, as contrasted with the pressing of extreme disagreements in *The General Theory* – that

'we have entirely freed ourselves – *this applies to every party and every quarter* – from the philosophy of the *laissez-faire* state'.

He added somewhat modestly and tentatively: 'Perhaps we know more'.

Keynes went on:

'Three years ago it was important to use public policy to increase investment. *It may soon be equally important to retard certain types of investment, so as to keep our most easily available ammunition in hand for when it is more required* . . . Just as it was advisable for the Government to incur debt during the slump, so for the same reasons *it is now advisable that they should incline to the opposite policy*. . . . Just as it was advisable for local authorities to press on with capital expenditure during the slump, so *it is now advisable that they should postpone whatever new enterprises can reasonably be held back*.'

Keynes then admitted that it might be considered premature to abate efforts to increase employment so long as the figures of unemployment remained so high – i.e. around 11-12 per cent. He explained, however:

'I believe that *we are approaching, or have reached, the point where there is not much advantage in applying a further general stimulus at the centre*. So long as surplus resources were widely diffused between industries and localities it was no great matter at what point in the economic structure the impulse of an increased demand was applied. But the evidence grows that – for several reasons into which there is no space to enter here – *the economic structure is unfortunately rigid*, and that (for example) building activity in the home counties is less effective than one might have hoped in decreasing unemployment in the distressed areas. *It follows that the later stages of recovery require a different technique*. . . .

We are in more need today of a rightly distributed demand than of a greater aggregate demand; and the Treasury would be entitled to economise

---

[1] All references in this section, unless otherwise stated, are to *The Times* of 1937. Italics have been added.

elsewhere to compensate for the cost of special assistance to the distressed areas.'

Rearmament expenditure

It should be noted that Keynes specifically and explicitly took account of rearmament expenditure (14 January, 1937):

'. . . sooner or later the building activity will relax; and *the cost of rearmament is neither permanent nor large enough while it lasts to sustain prosperity by itself* (in 1936 at least 7 or 8 times as much was spent on new building as on rearmament).'

Let us repeat that what Keynes was concerned with was not rearmament, but, as the title of his articles indicated, 'How to Avoid a Slump'. In a speech on 25 February, 1937, Keynes again stressed the damping down of aggregate demand. But although the government was now proposing to borrow £80 million per annum for defence purposes for five years, Keynes emphasised:

'I feel no doubt that the sums which the Chancellor of the Exchequer proposes to borrow are well within our capacity; *particularly if as much of the expenditure as possible is directed to bringing into employment the unused resources of the special areas. It is incumbent on the Government to have a concerted policy for retarding other postponable capital expenditure, particularly in the near future, if temporary congestion is to be avoided.*'

By 11 March, in an article headed 'Borrowing for Defence',[1] Keynes was maintaining:

'The Chancellor's loan expenditure *need* not be inflationary. But . . . *it may be rather near the limit.*[2] . . . *In two years' time, or less, rearmament loans may be positively helpful in warding off a depression. On the other hand, the War Departments may not succeed – they seldom do – in spending up to their time-table.*'

Keynes added:

'*It is most important that we should avoid war-time controls, rationing and the like.*'

---

[1] [Reproduced by kind permission of the Editor of *The Times* in Appendix B, pp. 74–77. – ED.]

[2] Sir John Hicks has written (in *The Crisis in Keynesian Economics*, Blackwell, 1974, p. 61): 'The view which emerges from *The General Theory* is more radical than "full employment without inflation"; it is nothing less than the view that inflation does not matter . . . The extreme position which he takes by implication in *The General Theory* is surely to be explained by the circumstances of its time. Inflation in 1936 seemed far from being a danger.' If inflation seemed far from being a danger in 1936, *by 1937 it was, for Keynes, by no means remote.* Keynes was doubtless much more flexible and quick on his feet than most of his followers.

He went on:

> '*The number of insured persons who are still unemployed is, indeed, as high as 12½ per cent . . . But though the new demand will be widely spread . . . we cannot safely regard even half of these unemployed insured persons as being available to satisfy home demand. For we have to subtract the unemployables, those seasonally unemployed, etc., and those who cannot readily be employed except in producing for export.*'

Counter-cyclical public works again

It should be emphasised that Keynes's proposals again amounted largely to the medicine as before, that is, counter-cyclical public works. He wanted a Board of Public Investment to prepare detailed schemes which could be put immediately into operation as required – a proposal which had appeared in the Liberal Yellow Book of 1928 and which Winston Churchill had advocated in 1908.

That Keynes's concern throughout 1937 was avoiding a slump is made absolutely clear in a letter to *The Times* of 28 December, in which he supported proposals for preparing schemes of public works against the next down-turn, when unemployment would be liable to rise again from the 11-12 per cent at which it then stood. He was engaged in attacking the arguments of those who were still clinging to the traditional Ricardian case against public works. Keynes asked whether it was being argued that:

> 'e.g. slum clearance and the improvement of transport facilities do not increase employment? Or that they are of no public benefit when made? Does he [Sir Charles Mallet, to whose letter of 18 December Keynes was replying] believe that the present rearmament expenditure, partly financed out of loans, has no effect on employment? Or is he supposing that there is some special virtue in instruments of destruction, so that expenditure on them helps employment, whereas an equal expenditure on, let us say, objects of public health would be of no use?
>
> If he disputes the view that public loan expenditure helps employment he is *running counter to the almost unanimous opinion of contemporary economists.*'

Keynes conceded that

> 'public loan expenditure is not, of course, the only way, *and not necessarily the best way to increase employment.*'

Again, however, he argued:

> 'It is very generally held today that there is a good deal of advantage

in retarding expenditure by such bodies when other sources of demand are strong. . . . This is probably a reason for *not pushing such expenditure at present.*'

On 3 January, 1938, Keynes again emphasised the overwhelming weight of opinion in favour of public works against unemployment, which policy, he maintained, was bound to be adopted when the next depression came:

> 'The weight both of authority and of public opinion in favour of meeting a recession in employment by organised loan expenditure is now so great that *this policy is practically certain to be adopted when the time comes.*'

By March 1938, with Hitler's reorganisation of his high command and the annexation of Austria, the international situation had clearly moved into a new and much grimmer phase. But what emerges clearly from these writings of Keynes in 1937, his last under fully peace-time assumptions, is that his ideas about how far unemployment could or should be reduced simply by additional government spending, and about the dangers of inflation, differed vastly from the doctrines on these subjects on behalf of which his magic name came to be invoked, or which came to be described and advocated as 'Keynesian', or 'neo-Keynesian', in the 1950s and 1960s. For in 1937 Keynes was clearly concerned with the *possible dangers of inflation when unemployment was still around 11-12 per cent.* From that level downwards Keynes insisted that unemployment must be dealt with, *not by the general expansion of aggregate demand by government (or by 'a further general stimulus at the centre'), but by 'a different technique'*: that is, by specific measures in the depressed areas.

With unemployment still at 11-12 per cent, Keynes was urging the damping down of extra public borrowing and deficits. *This does not, of course, imply that Keynes did not think that unemployment would and should come down to a lower level,* but that he was relying on the further impetus of the boom in the private sector and on the adoption of the 'different technique'.

Keynes's approach to the 'natural rate of unemployment' concept
In fact, Keynes can be said to have suggested a similar concept to that now called – following Professor Milton Friedman – a 'natural rate' of unemployment in that he stressed 'the unfortunately rigid' elements in the British economy which made it undesirable to try

to reduce unemployment further by the expansion of central government demand. It is not, of course, maintained that Keynes held to a clear and consistent concept of the natural rate, or that these articles spell out the doctrine of a natural rate of unemployment as clearly as it came to be understood in the 1970s. But Keynes's writings of 1937 clearly suggest that attempts to bring unemployment down below a certain level by more and more of what he called a 'general stimulus at the centre', may constitute a disastrous mistake.[1]

During the war, when unemployment had been reduced to below 1 per cent, Keynes was apparently prepared to suggest about $4\frac{1}{2}$ per cent unemployment as an equilibrium level for peace-time. But he was sceptical about the feasibility of the Beveridge target of 3 per cent.[2] Anyhow, these estimates were all obviously based on the fundamental principle which he firmly proclaimed in the House of Lords (in May 1944) that: '*We intend to prevent inflation at home.*'

Moreover, it must be emphasised that during the war, in discussing figures like $4\frac{1}{2}$ or 3 per cent, Keynes was simply speculating about general, more or less hypothetical, target figures. His last operational peace-time policy-proposals regarding a current employment target were those of 1937.

We would conclude this section by noting that we have not been calling attention simply to a single paragraph, nor even

---

[1] Keynes's views in his *Times* articles of January 1937 were the same as those of the Committee on Economic Information (of which he was a leading member) in its report of February 1937. The Committee maintained: 'We can no longer anticipate that the stimulus to economic activity generally associated with an increase in investment will make any substantial impression on the remaining volume of unemployment . . . Apart from the special areas *the postponement of such investment activity as is not of an urgent character would, on balance, prove beneficial to the average level of employment over a period of years* . . . Our first recommendation is therefore that the government should take what steps are possible to postpone work upon investment projects which are not of an urgent character.' (S. Howson and D. Winch, *The Economic Advisory Council 1930-1939*, CUP, 1977, p. 346.) It is not clear whether Lord Kahn would apply his explanation of Keynes's views to the simultaneous recommendations of the Committee on Economic Information.

[2] By the middle of 1939 Keynes was maintaining that 'the end of abnormal unemployment was in sight', with the total at about $1\frac{1}{2}$ million and a further reduction of at least half-a-million forecast for the end of the year. But then it was a twilight period of mobilisation between peace and impending war, so that conclusions about Keynes's views on peace-time normality cannot be drawn. (*The Times*, 17 April and 24-25 July, 1939, and *The Listener*, 1 June, 1939; also my *Economics and Economic Policy* . . ., *op. cit.*, p. 298.)

to a single article, which might represent an aberration, but to views expressed over a period of a year in a number of articles and letters. Furthermore, we would emphasise still further that we are not, of course, suggesting that Keynes, had he lived, would have necessarily held to exactly the same views in 1957 or 1967 as he expressed in 1937. We are simply insisting that it is quite unjustifiable to proclaim as 'Keynesian', or 'neo-Keynesian', views which conflict seriously with those which Keynes expressed in some of his last relevant pronouncements.

IV. Keynes and the Pseudo-Keynesians

The doctrines of Keynes set out in his articles of 1937 obviously conflict very seriously with the Pseudo-Keynesian views regarding employment policy and its objectives developed in the 1950s and 1960s. Anyhow, his attention having been called to these statements of Keynes, Lord Kahn seems to have regarded them as requiring some kind of explanation, since a perfectly clear and straightforward interpretation of them was so completely unacceptable to the new 'Keynesian' orthodoxy.[1]

'Mystery' or misstatement?

Lord Kahn found that Keynes's articles 'convey a curious impression', and indeed constitute a 'mystery', which, however, he claimed, *'was soon cleared up'* by the explanations he offered. He began by stating that Keynes

'did not in these articles mention the needs of rearmament.'[2]

This statement is quite incorrect. We have just (Chapter III) quoted two or three explicit references by Keynes to rearmament and could have quoted more. One of his articles (11 March) was headed 'Borrowing for Defence'. Keynes was explicitly taking the needs of rearmament into account. Lord Kahn then goes on to explain the non-fact of Keynes's omission to mention rearmament as

'prompted by political strategy. The time was not quite ripe.

It is my belief that Keynes was anxious that a considerable reserve army of unemployed be maintained to meet the demands of the drastic stepping up of the rearmament programme . . . as well as the highly probable demand for recruits into the armed forces.'

What Lord Kahn is inviting his readers, including admirers of

---

[1] 'What Keynes Really Said', *Sunday Telegraph*, 22 September, 1974; also his 'Unemployment as seen by the Keynesians', in G. D. N. Worswick (ed.), *The Concept and Measurement of Involuntary Unemployment*, Allen & Unwin, 1976, pp. 27-34.

[2] *Ibid.*

Keynes, to believe is, *first*, that Keynes was guilty of duplicity towards the British public in that he *pretended* that he was concerned with avoiding the next slump, and the unemployment it would bring, when really *he was anxious to maintain 'a considerable reserve army of unemployed'*. Obviously anyone who sees Keynes as a man who believed above all in open, frank, and rational debate is, according to Lord Kahn, profoundly mistaken in this case.

Secondly, admirers of Keynes are invited by Lord Kahn to believe that Keynes was 'anxious' to maintain 'a considerable reserve army of unemployed', *for an indefinite period;* since it must be remembered that in 1937 it was very unclear when, whether, or how many armament workers and recruits for the forces would be required. But Keynes intended, according to Lord Kahn, that 'considerable' numbers of men should be kept out of work for an indefinite period, *who otherwise could readily have been put into jobs* – although if military exigencies later became pressing these men could have moved, or even been conscripted, into defence work or the services.[1]

It is quite extraordinary, both to attribute to Keynes concealment of motives on some theory of 'political strategy' and 'unripe time', as well as to ascribe to him an anxiety to maintain a reserve army of unemployed *for an indefinite period and for no economic reason.*

Keynes and Lord Kahn on an unemployed reserve

Also completely unexplained by Lord Kahn are Keynes's repeated warnings in 1937 regarding a forthcoming slump and unemployment – *in spite of rearmament* – and his repeated demands for the preparation of plans for *civilian* public works, such as *'slum clearance and the improvement of transport facilities'* (28 December, 1937). It is not clear why Keynes was so repeatedly expressing these worries about combating unemployment *in the next slump*, when 'we shall be hard put to it, in my opinion, to develop useful activities on an adequate scale', if what he was really concerned with was *the maintenance, for no economic reason, of 'a considerable reserve army of unemployed'*. That it was all, throughout a whole year, an elaborate

---

[1] Even Winston Churchill was proclaiming, on 15 September, 1937: 'I declare my belief that a major war is not imminent, and I still believe there is a good chance of no major war taking place in our time': quoted by A. J. P. Taylor, *Beaverbrook*, Hamish Hamilton, 1972, p. 375. Mr Taylor adds: 'Nowadays it is too easily believed that there was a steady slide towards war from 1931 to 1939'.

public deception, 'prompted by political strategy', is simply not credible. In fact Keynes was claiming that 'in two years' time, or less, rearmament loans may be positively helpful *in warding off a depression*' and that the War Department would not 'spend up to their time-table'.

Perhaps it may appear that all that Lord Kahn's 'explanation' of Keynes's writing in 1937 does really explain, are the extreme lengths to which 'Keynesians' are prepared to proceed in trying to explain away the wide divergence between Keynes's views on employment policies and objectives and the Pseudo-Keynesian orthodoxies which became the conventional unwisdom of the 1950s and 1960s.[1] The perfectly clear and straight-forward meaning of Keynes's articles of 1937 – not to mention the parallel recommendations of the Committee on Economic Information of which he was a leading member–demonstrates that this divergence is very wide indeed.

'A nonsense question'?

Lord Kahn concluded his account entitled 'What Keynes Really Said' with the assertion that:

> 'Had Keynes survived for some considerable number of years, I believe that in the light of post-war experience he would have aimed at an appreciably more ambitious full employment target, but would have regarded . . . 2·2 per cent unemployed . . . as unduly low.'

All that should be said is: 'Perhaps so, perhaps not'. But it is certainly unjustifiable to imply that the views on employment targets and policies which came to be described as 'Keynesian', in the 1950s and 1960s, were those held by Keynes, or that they would have been approved by Keynes had he lived. Moreover, Lord Kahn is here certainly not telling us 'What Keynes Really Said'; while his assertion also conflicts with his cautious statement elsewhere that:

---

[1] Professor Moggridge, the leading authority on the Keynes papers, has remarked that he has 'not as yet come across sufficient evidence to support' Lord Kahn's 'construction'. (D. E. Moggridge, *Keynes,* Macmillan, 1976, p. 177.) But there is much more than sufficient evidence to *refute* Lord Kahn's 'construction', if one assumes that there has always been much more than sufficient evidence to refute the proposition that Keynes was a purveyor of elaborate and self-contradictory public deceptions.

'The question what Keynes would be advocating today is, of course, a nonsense question.'[1]

However, as we shall see, Lord Kahn himself, together with Sir Roy Harrod and Joan (Lady) Robinson, had, for years past, been laying down the answers to just such 'nonsense' questions with the utmost confidence.

---

[1] *On Re-Reading Keynes,* British Academy, 1975, p. 32.

V. Keynes's Approach to Post-War Economic Policy

For an appreciation of the general principles of economic policy with which, at the time of his death, Keynes was approaching the problems of the post-war world, his last, posthumously published article, 'The Balance of Payments of the United States', is obviously of major interest and importance.[1]

In this article Keynes came to the conclusion that, although he was prepared to resort to 'exchange variation and overall import controls', we *'would need such expedients less if the classical medicine is also at work'*.

'The wisdom of Adam Smith'

In fact Keynes did not regard it as necessary or desirable to rely primarily or predominantly on government controls, which must be used, as he put it, 'not to defeat but to implement the wisdom of Adam Smith'. He maintained:

> 'I find myself moved, not for the first time, to remind contemporary economists that the classical teaching embodied some permanent truths of great significance . . .
>
> There are in these matters deep undercurrents at work, natural forces, one can call them, or even the invisible hand, which are operating towards equilibrium . . . If we reject the medicine from our systems altogether, we may just drift on from expedient to expedient and never get really fit again.'

Finally, Keynes deplored how much 'modernist stuff, gone wrong and turned sour and silly, is circulating'. The proclamation of these guidelines, or principles, of wide generality, were virtually Keynes's final words as an economist. It seems difficult to deny how profoundly and acutely distasteful they must have been to some of the Keynesian *entourage*.

---

[1] *Economic Journal*, June 1946, pp. 172 ff.

Keynes's views on the post-war dollar 'shortage'
Lord Kahn subsequently (1956) complained that this last article of Keynes was written in a 'more than usually optimistic vein, and also in a strangely complacent vein'.[1] This may have referred to Keynes's excessive short-run optimism regarding dollar-shortage.[2] But surely Keynes was *much less* wide of the mark regarding long-run dollar prospects, on which policies should have been based, than the various enthusiasts for government regulation who went on predicting a disastrous dollar shortage as a chronic, *permanent*, world problem right up to when the 'shortage' was becoming a massive surplus.[3] Anyhow, Keynes certainly did not show himself in the least optimistic or complacent about the effectiveness of government controls over trade or wages, regarding which Pseudo-Keynesians were to be so persistently over-optimistic in the ensuing decades.

Keynes's 'prophetic instincts'
However, by 1974 Lord Kahn was prepared to admit that Keynes 'did display prophetic instincts' in this last article. But Lord Kahn went on:

> 'It is less obvious that Keynes was justified in his remarkable belief in the efficacy of "deep undercurrents at work, natural forces, one can call them, or even the invisible hand, which are operating towards equilibrium". Keynes, a sick man, was displaying a natural irritation over "modernist stuff gone wrong and turned sour and silly".'[4]

But *who* can Keynes have been getting at in these famous words? Anyhow, it is perhaps permissible to suggest that in subsequent decades it would have been only 'a sick man' who would *not* very

---

[1] *Selected Essays on Employment and Growth*, CUP, 1972, p. 123.
[2] On this point, too, Keynes's views have been distorted. Lord Balogh has asserted: 'Keynes wrote in his last article that . . . the Americans would prove a high-living and high-spending country and that the balance of world trade would be restored in the next two years.' This is a falsehood. There is no mention whatsoever of 'the next two years' in Keynes's article, and his justified prediction that 'the United States is becoming a high-living, high-cost country beyond any previous experience', referred specifically to 'the long run'. (v. *Keynes and International Monetary Relations*, A. P. Thirlwall (ed)., Macmillan, 1976, p. 98, and *Economic Journal*, June 1946, p. 185.)
[3] Opinions on the dollar 'shortage' in the 1940s and 1950s are quoted in Hutchison, *Economics and Economic Policy* . . ., *op. cit.*, pp. 44-9, 96-8, and 161-5. Lord Balogh continued periodically to proclaim a dollar 'shortage' throughout the 'fifties down, at least, until 1958. (v. *Oxford Economic Papers*, June 1958, p. 235.)
[4] *On Re-reading Keynes, op. cit.*, p. 23n.

frequently have felt irritated over 'modernist stuff, gone wrong
and turned sour and silly' – surely one of Keynes's truly prophetic
phrases.[1]

Certainly it is very easy to understand, from the passages we have
quoted from Keynes's last article, the complaint of Joan Robinson
that some 'Keynesians'

> 'sometimes had some trouble in getting Maynard to see what the point
> of his revolution really was'.[2]

No wonder Keynes is reported, in the last year of his life, as saying:
'I am not a Keynesian'.[3] In fact, it might appear that Keynes
himself was rather a 'bastard Keynesian' – to apply the genealogical
certification so magisterially proclaimed by Joan Robinson.[4]

---

[1] Regarding this last posthumously published article of Keynes the late Professor
Jacob Viner, perhaps the greatest economist-scholar of his day, remarked how far
it 'startled his disciples by its optimistic tone, and there was serious consideration
of the desirability of suppressing it'. Viner's suggestion, valid or invalid, is
quite extraordinary. Equally extraordinary is the notion that the suppression of
Keynes's article was desirable in order to ensure that the US Congress approved the
Loan Agreement – as was discussed with a Treasury official. (Kahn, in A. P.
Thirlwall (ed.), *Keynes and International Monetary Relations, op. cit.,* p. 8; and
R. Lekachman (ed.), *Keynes' General Theory: Reports of Three Decades*, St. Martin's,
N.Y., and Macmillan, 1964, p. 265.) According to Joan Robinson: 'At the
end of his life, feeling obliged to defend the Bretton Woods agreement against
his better judgement (Kahn, 1976), he lapsed into arguing that, *in the long run,*
market forces would tend to establish equilibrium in international trade (Keynes,
1946).' (J. Robinson and F. Wilkinson, 'What has become of employment policy?',
Cambridge Journal of Economics, March 1977, p. 10, and Kahn, *op. cit.*)

[2] 'What has Become of the Keynesian Revolution?', in Milo Keynes (ed.), *Essays
on J. M. Keynes, op. cit.,* p. 125.

[3] Colin Clark, *Taxmanship*, Hobart Paper 26, IEA, 2nd edn., 1970, p. 53.

[4] The most recent pronouncements of Joan Robinson leave little room for doubt
that Keynes was, in her terms, a 'bastard Keynesian'. For example, according to
Joan Robinson: 'The bastard Keynesians turned the argument back into being
a defence of *laissez-faire* provided that just one blemish of excessive saving was
going to be removed.' Given Joan Robinson's meaning of *laissez-faire*, this
'bastard Keynesian' argument seems to be a succint but reasonably accurate summary
of the Concluding Notes of *The General Theory*. In fact, according to Joan Robinson,
Pigou (though recognising exceptions) regarded *laissez-faire* as 'a rule which in
general could not be questioned'; while Keynes agreed (1937) that 'when it comes
to practice, there is really extremely little' between himself and Pigou. (v. *An Introduc-
tion to Modern Economics*, 1973, p. 47, and *Collected Writings of J. M. Keynes*, vol. 14,
1973, p. 259.)

VI. Pseudo-Keynesian Doctrines: Full Employment without Inflation

We turn now to the emergence, in the two decades after Keynes's death, of Pseudo-Keynesian doctrines, drastically differing from those of Keynes, regarding employment objectives and the dangers of inflation.[1]

With the proclamation in 1944 of 'a high and stable level of employment'[2] as an agreed objective of economic policy, there was, for a very short time, a notable measure of caution and moderation regarding the level of employment which it was sensible, feasible, or desirable to aim at. There seemed, very briefly, to be some realisation of the dangers of pushing policies directed against the social injustice of unemployment so far as to incur the serious risk of releasing other acute sources of social injustice, such as inflation or the restriction of freedoms. Pigou, for example, had observed that the result of maintaining a very high level of employment might be that

'a spiralling movement of inflation is allowed to develop.'[3]

Kaldor on Beveridge's 3 per cent objective
Lord Kaldor in 1944 went so far as to assert that Beveridge's full employment objective of 3 per cent would (and should) be combined *with price stability*. He assumed:

'that post-war governments will pursue a monetary and wage policy which maintains the prices of final commodities constant . . .'

Lord Kaldor then cautiously added:

---

[1] An earlier and shorter version of the following paragraphs may be found in the latter part of my paper to Section F of the British Association, 1975, reprinted in Aubrey Jones (ed.), *Economics and Equality*, Philip Allan, 1976, pp. 58-63.

[2] *Employment Policy*, Cmd. 6527, HMSO, May 1944, p. 3.

[3] *Lapses from Full Employment*, Macmillan, 1944, p. 72; also other similar quotations cited in Hutchison, *Economics and Economic Policy . . ., op. cit.*, pp. 28-30.

'A policy of a rising price level might be incompatible with the maintenance of stability in the long run.'[1]

Also among the assumptions of Beveridge's 3 per cent target was not only the pursuit of price stability, but compulsory arbitration, and that:

> 'In peace in a free society, men should not be imprisoned for striking, though they may rightly be deprived of all support if the strike is contrary to a collective bargain or an agreed arbitration.'[2]

But the dangers of the pursuit of the full employment objective creating injustices, or loss of freedom in other directions, were, perhaps, most incisively insisted upon by Joan Robinson. In a paper of 1946 she argued:

> 'Nor is completely full employment desirable. The attainment of full employment, in this absolute sense, would require strict controls, including direction of labour. To raise the average of employment from 86 per cent (the average for Great Britain 1921-38) to, say, 95 per cent would be compatible with a greater amount of individual liberty than to raise it from 95 per cent to 98 per cent. To raise it from 95 per cent to 98 per cent (not momentarily – but on the average) would involve great sacrifices of liberty, and to raise it from 98 per cent to 100 per cent would involve complete conscription of labour. No-one regards 100 per cent employment as a desirable objective.'[3]

One may not today agree with the precise estimate of the trade-offs as they were envisaged in the 1940s by Joan Robinson, and it is not clear whose – or what kinds of – 'freedom' she held to be threatened by reducing unemployment to 2 or even 5 per cent. But one must certainly admire her cautious and discerning insistence on the serious costs, or the various forms of injustice, or loss of freedom, which the pursuit of very high levels of employment might entail.

Cautious and conditional approach short-lived

Thus when, in the 1940s, the revolutionary attempt was launched

---

[1] See Appendix C to W. Beveridge, *Full Employment in a Free Society*, Allen & Unwin, 1944, p. 398.

[2] *Ibid.*, p. 200.

[3] *Collected Economic Papers*, Blackwell, 1951, p. 106 (italics added). Also *Essays in the Theory of Employment*, 2nd edn., 1947, p. 26: 'In general it may be said that something appreciably short of full employment must be regarded as the optimum'. (Italics added.)

at 'full' employment in peace-time, three conditions in particular were set out by people claiming to be followers of Keynes regarding:

(1) trade unions and the right to strike (Beveridge);
(2) the importance of price stability (Kaldor); and
(3) the preservation of freedom (J. Robinson).

When Keynes remarked that there was 'no harm in trying' for Beveridge's 3 per cent target (though he doubted whether it was attainable), it must be assumed that Keynes placed at least as much weight on the conditions regarding strikes and price stability as had Beveridge and Kaldor. Nor is it reasonable to assume that Keynes would have rejected less firmly than Joan Robinson any great 'sacrifices of liberty'. One can also surely be confident that Keynes would not have forgotton or surrendered on these conditions because they began to run counter to fashionable opinion or were unpalatable to the trade union bosses.

For after Keynes's death all this caution and moderation turned out to be very short-lived. By the early or middle 1950s the trend of public taste for bursts of very high employment, and the politicians' eagerness to meet these tastes – *regardless of losses or dangers in other directions* – had become clear. One could not hope to keep one's place on the trendy political bandwagon if one nagged away about price-stability and the dangers to freedom of over-full employment. Keynes himself would surely have had to endure the most appalling vituperation in 1957 if he had then repeated the kind of views about employment targets which he had expressed in 1937. (But one may assume that Keynes would not have been concerned about his popularity with politicians of one stripe or another.) 'Growthmanship' also was beginning to emerge at this stage, and a body of doctrine began to achieve a dominating influence which may be described as 'Pseudo-Keynesian'. For, while the Master's magic name was frequently invoked on behalf of the new conventional unwisdom, *it is impossible to find statements of these new doctrines in Keynes's writings.*

Four Pseudo-Keynesian doctrines

Four main Pseudo-Keynesian doctrines may be distinguished; there are no grounds for supposing that Keynes would have supported any of them:

(i) *Higher than safe employment via demand expansion*
The first was that by expanding aggregate demand the unemployment percentage should be pushed down to levels well below those that had been regarded by Keynes as safely attainable.

Lord Kahn, for example, in 1956, simply proclaimed the Beveridge target of 3 per cent as 'obsolete';[1] while Joan Robinson (1966) stated that any target above 2 per cent was 'cold-blooded' and 'out of the question'.[2] The great sacrifices of liberty which had been discerned in 1946 as required by such low levels of unemployment were now left unmentioned. Sir Roy Harrod wanted a *zero* target for unemployment. In an article in the *New Statesman* (1969), entitled 'The Arrested Revolution', Sir Roy claimed *absolutely certain knowledge* about Keynes's views on employment targets:

> 'People sometimes say to me that what worried Keynes was the massive unemployment of pre-war days. Surely he would not object to raising unemployment from 1·5 to 2·5 per cent in this country or from 3·3 per cent to 4 per cent in the USA if, as so many are now urging, that cured the external deficits of those countries? . . . *He certainly would object.*'[3]

There is no doubt about the popularity of such arguments with politicians and public. But the possibility that by pushing down unemployment in the short term, by government expansion of aggregate demand, one was likely only to *increase* it seriously in the long term – or to bring about totalitarianism – was something which Sir Roy was unable or unwilling to contemplate. Nor can it easily be explained how the views of Sir Roy, which he attributed to Keynes, are compatible with the proposals which Keynes put forward in his articles of 1937, either as interpreted straightforwardly or even according to the 'explanation' of Lord Kahn. Indeed by 1977 Lord Kahn was admitting that, since the end of the war:

> 'There have been periods in which employment has been *considerably above the level which Keynes would have advocated.*'[4]

Precisely. But surely, then, the genuine 'Keynesians' must have

---

[1] *Selected Essays on Employment and Growth, op. cit.*, p. 102.
[2] *Economics: An Awkward Corner*, Allen & Unwin, 1966, p. 20.
[3] *New Statesman*, 5 December, 1969, p. 809.
[4] *Lloyds Bank Review*, April 1977, p. 3 (italics added).

been those who, from time to time, have had the courage, as Keynes presumably would have had, to attack over-full employment – like Sir Dennis Robertson, Lord Robbins and others; while the 'Pseudo'-Keynesians have been those who in 30 years have repeatedly called for higher and higher employment percentages and have at no time come out against the pushing up of employment *'considerably above the level which Keynes would have advocated'.*

(ii) *'Full growth' objective*

On the top of the full employment objective, pushed much further than Keynes approved, the objective of 'full growth', or 'growth in accordance with maximum potential', was to be adopted.

Sir Roy Harrod (1964) asserted that this new objective was

'supported by many economists who would claim to have drawn their inspiration from Keynes. . . . *I have no doubt at all that Keynes himself, were he alive . . . would be an ardent apostle of growth policies.'*[1]

Lord Kaldor (1959 and 1963) proclaimed that the rate of growth of the British economy could and should be raised by 'comprehensive planning' and 'purposive direction'.[2] Joan Robinson (1964) maintained:

'We could evidently quickly work up to 6 or 7 per cent [rate of growth] if Britain abandoned her defence effort.'[3]

Of course, hardly a vestige can be found in the later, rather stagnationist, writings of Keynes of this kind of Pseudo-Keynesian growthmanship (in spite of Sir Roy Harrod, in 1964, having *'no doubt at all'* of Keynes's 'ardent' support).

(iii) *Reduced price-stability objective*

The third Pseudo-Keynesian policy doctrine was that price-stability must have a minor or reduced priority as an objective.

After a decade in which prices in Britain had already risen almost unprecedentedly fast by full peace-time standards, Lord Kaldor warned the Radcliffe Committee (1959) of 'The Dangers of a Régime of Stable Prices'.[4] Apparently Lord Kaldor had dismissed

---

[1] *Encounter*, January 1964, p. 47 (italics added).
[2] *Encounter*, March 1963, p. 63, and *Essays on Economic Policy*, Duckworth, Vol. I, 1964, p. 199.
[3] *Collected Economic Papers*, Vol. III, 1965, p. 146.
[4] *Essays on Economic Policy*, Vol. I, 1964, p. 137.

as 'obsolete' his emphasis of 1944 on how a policy of a rising price-level might be incompatible with economic stability in the long run. Lord Kahn also affirmed to the Radcliffe Committee that even advocating the merits of absolute price stability was 'highly prejudicial to the country's interests'. He also asserted:

> 'In the absence of anything like what might be called a wages policy, it would, I am convinced, be economically expedient, as well as politically inevitable, *to abandon any idea of stability of the price level.*'[1]

(iv) *Incomes policies to counter inflation*
Fourthly, it was maintained that any tendencies to inflation could and should be countered mainly or entirely by wages or incomes policies.

Lord Kahn informed the Radcliffe Committee:

> 'It would, I submit, be a grave mistake for the Committee to accept the view that it is the proper function of monetary and budgetary policy to secure a tolerable behaviour of prices. One can readily admit the advantages of a stable price level taken in isolation. *It does not follow – very far from it – that the right aim of monetary policy is to secure a stable price level.* The real solution lies elsewhere. It lies in the realm of wage negotiations.'[2]

In practice, according to Joan Robinson, stating what she described as 'A Neo-Keynesian View':*'Incomes policy is the only real remedy'.*[3]

However, there seemed to be wide disagreements among Keynesians, as we shall see (Chapter VII), on what the role of trade unions had been, or might be, or as to how they might be expected to play their part – vital questions if sole reliance for averting inflation was being placed on 'incomes policy'. We may simply

---

[1] *Committee on the Working of the Monetary System, Principal Memoranda of Evidence,* Vol. 3, HMSO, 1960, p. 143 (italics added).
  Lord Kahn has subsequently referred to the 'fifties as 'a period of very modest inflation' (*Lloyds Bank Review*, April 1977, p. 11). On the other hand, the Radcliffe Committee prudently warned at the time: 'Nobody has lost sight of – indeed nobody has been allowed to lose sight of – the disadvantages of instability in the internal and external value of money. The rise in the cost of living has been a constant embarrassment to Governments and by 1957 the more ominous phrase "falling value of money" was constantly used.' (*Radcliffe Report*, 1959, p. 18.)

[2] *Op. cit.,* 1960, p. 143. As Mr Eltis has noticed, Lord Kahn also advised the Radcliffe Committee regarding budgetary policy: 'To my mind, the "overall" deficit is of no significance'. (Kahn, *op. cit.,* p. 145; and Eltis, *Lloyds Bank Review*, October 1976, p. 18.)

[3] 'Inflation and Stabilisation, a *Neo-Keynesian* View', *Spectator,* 19 October, 1974, p. 488 (italics added).

note that the growthmanship doctrines of how the growth-rate in Britain could and should be significantly raised, or doubled, by 'purposive planning', etc., combined with the advocacy of a rising price-level and the abandonment of price-stability, were obviously calculated to encourage the militant stepping-up of wage claims.

Pseudo-Keynesian doctrines and public expenditure

Pseudo-Keynesian doctrines, explicitly invoking the name of Keynes, were also widely disseminated in non-specialist political journalism. In particular was this so with what could be regarded as a further Pseudo-Keynesian doctrine which maintained that because, in the 1930s, Keynes had advocated public expenditure against unemployment, therefore *any cuts in public expenditure, in virtually any circumstances, must be anti-Keynesian, or a betrayal of Keynes's teachings.* For example, when in February 1976, with a public sector deficit of around £10,000 million, and a heavy adverse balance of payments, the Labour Government was putting forward some (partly illusory) public expenditure 'cuts', the *New Statesman* proclaimed:[1]

> 'It is exactly 40 years since Keynes produced *The General Theory* and half a century since he wrote *The End of Laissez-Faire*. . . . The Government's White Paper reads as if . . . [they] had never been written.'

Ten years previously, in July 1966, with unemployment at a record peace-time 'low' of about 1·1 per cent, a Labour Government had also engaged in 'cuts', regarding which the columnist of *Encounter* inquired whether it was not the case

> 'that the Government, and the Labour Party, have now flung Keynes to the winds and that, in the advanced economic thought of today, Keynes has been superseded by Callaghan, with his eternal Micawber verity that a country in the red is necessarily ruined?'[2]

Regarding the 1966 crisis, the diaries of the Rt Hon R. H. S. Crossman provide an interesting example of Pseudo-Keynesian doctrines being pressed upon Ministers as expert 'briefing'. Shortly after the crisis, Mr Crossman describes how he sought advice from the economic staff of the Prime Minister's 'kitchen cabinet':

> 'I've been thinking of a speech in which I could suggest that the thirties'

---

[1] 20 February, 1976, p. 211.

[2] *Encounter*, January 1967, p. 53.

crisis was a Keynesian crisis of demand failure whereas the crisis of the sixties was caused by full employment and the resulting excess demand and inflation. Michael taught me in a severe tutorial that *it's politically dangerous to talk about inflation in this way as a disease of the economy.* The real contrast, he says, is between the "demand-pull" failure in consumer demand in the 1930s which could have been solved by Keynesian methods of stimulating expenditure and the new crisis of "cost-push" and stunted economic growth in the 1960s. If I stress the notion of inflation I'm failing to realise that inflation is not a disease comparable to mass unemployment; indeed inflation has certain advantages as part of a process of economic growth.'[1]

It is obviously not fair to put all the blame on the politicians for the neglect of the dangers of inflation, when what was being impressed on them by their 'Keynesian' advisers was not the dangers of inflation but *the dangers of talking about inflation as a disease. Anyhow, in the production of this crucially influential climate of opinion among politicians and public, in the 1960s and early 1970s, the invocation of the charismatic name of Keynes was a persistent leitmotif.*

---

[1] *The Diaries of a Cabinet Minister*, Vol. II: *Lord President of the Council and Leader of the House of Commons 1966-68*, Hamish Hamilton and Jonathan Cape, 1976, p. 41 (italics added). 'Michael' is Mr Michael Stewart, author of the Pelican textbook, *Keynes and After*, Penguin Books, 1967 (2nd edn. 1972).

VII. The Role of the Trade Unions

Regarding the role of trade unions, the spirit of Keynes must often have felt like the Almighty in war-time, being invoked or appealed to by all the warring parties. But this is a subject of special importance in view of the emergence in the 1960s and 1970s of the trade union leaders as a kind of new power-élite. Anyhow, some versions of Pseudo-Keynesian conventional wisdom invoke Keynes's name for a comprehensive apologia on behalf of the trade union leaders, denying in the strongest terms that they have any responsibility for unemployment.[1] At the first Keynes Seminar held at the University of Kent, Mr R. Opie proclaimed:

> '*Keynes exonerated the trade unions. Unemployment is not high because wages are too high.* . . . Wage cuts alone will not cure unemployment, nor do wage increases cause it. In passing, one might note an extraordinary revival of this wage-cut doctrine in the pronouncements of Her Majesty's present Ministers. We have been told frequently that the record levels of unemployment were due to the record rate of price inflation, and that in turn is due to the record rate of wage inflation. The implication was not that wage cuts would restore full employment. That would no doubt be a little too crude – but a more subtle "first derivative" argument, *viz.* that a cut in the rate of wage *increases* will do the trick. We have, fortunately, heard less of this antediluvian argument since Mr Barber's latest expansionary budget, and *I expect we shall now hear no more of it at all.*'[2]

---

[1] We agree with Mr Tim Congdon that, generally speaking, 'The Keynesians are somewhat ambivalent in their attitude to the union movement,' but not that 'an insistence on the villainy of trade unions is, however, common to all the Keynesians . . .'. ('Are We Really All Keynesians Now?', *Encounter*, April 1975, p. 34.) Anyhow, 'Keynesians' have tended to support strongly the various restrictionist demands of the trade union leaders for import controls and for staying out of the European Economic Community.

[2] R. Opie, in D. E. Moggridge (ed.), *Keynes: Aspects of the Man and his Work, The First Keynes Seminar held at the University of Kent at Canterbury, 1972*, Macmillan, 1974, pp. 80 -1 (italics added).

'Tragic situation'

In fact, *very much* more was soon heard, in most emphatic, or even 'antediluvian', terms from the supreme 'Keynesian' authority, Lord Kahn, who insisted, with much indignation, on the gross culpability of the unions and their leaders and on the disastrous results of their policies:

> 'The result has been a crazily high rate of increase of money wages. *Unemployment results partly directly and partly because the Governor of the Bank of England feels compelled to adopt restrictive measures . . .*
>
> Trade union leaders must accept responsibility for this . . . They carry on their shoulders responsibility for a tragic situation.'

In a further contribution Lord Kahn referred to

> 'the astonishing stupidity of our trade union leaders,'

and to

> 'their complete failure to take a long-sighted view.'

The men who run the TUC, Lord Kahn asserted, 'are sadly lacking in intelligence'.[1]

Lord Kahn did not volunteer to explain how he had come to entertain either the hopes he had indulged in for so long regarding the prospects for negotiating agreements on incomes policies with people of such 'astonishing stupidity', or the visions which in 1958 he had commended to the Radcliffe Committee regarding:

> 'a considerable improvement in the state of awareness of the importance of restraint over wage increase.'[2]

In 1976, however, Lord Kahn went on to contrast the English unions with those of the German Federal Republic:

> 'Western Germany provides the best example of trade-union leaders who are long-sighted and who, as a result of modesty in the size of their claims for wage increases . . . have secured an economic climate conducive to productive investment and the growth of productivity.'[3]

---

[1] *New Statesman*, 1 August, 1975, p. 142; and *Lloyds Bank Review*, January 1976, pp. 4–5. It is interesting to contrast Lord Kahn's pronouncements on the trade union leaders with his fellow 'Keynesian', Sir Roy Harrod's, confidence that a national wage agreement could be reached 'given a guarantee of price stability', because 'many trade union leaders are good economists'. (*The Times*, 21 July, 1976.) Lord Kahn also leaves unexplained his doctrine that monetary policy must always be so permissively framed as to exclude *any* unemployment, however 'crazily' high wages are pushed by leaders of such 'astonishing stupidity'.

[2] *Committee on the Working of the Monetary System, Principal Memoranda of Evidence, op. cit.*, p. 143.

[3] 'Thoughts on the behaviour of wages and monetarism', *Lloyds Bank Review*, January 1976, p. 5.

This is an especially interesting comparison because, as long ago as
1950, when Dr Erhardt was launching out on free market policies,
Lord Balogh castigated the 'obsolete' and 'iniquitous' policies of
Dr Erhardt's 'satellite economists' who were, he alleged, trying to
discredit *'enlightened Keynesian economic policy'*. Lord Balogh
maintained:

> 'The currency reform helped to weaken the trade unions. They cannot
> and do not press with decisive force for more decent working and social
> conditions. Their weakness may even inhibit increases in productivity.'[1]

The 'arrested (Keynesian) revolution'?

Leading 'Keynesians', of different political inclinations, have
tended to protest vehemently that the Keynesian 'revolution' was
never properly completed. Joan Robinson, for example, asked
(1972), 'What has become of the Keynesian Revolution?'; while
Sir Roy Harrod (1969) referred to 'The Arrested Revolution'.[2]
What seems to have been meant was that Joan Robinson and
Sir Roy had not always been one hundred per cent successful in
selling as 'Keynesian' the particular nostrums they favoured.
*Moreover, 'Keynesian' economists, through the 'fifties and 'sixties,
constantly expressed and encouraged discontent with employment levels
in Britain.*

On the whole, however, what Lord Balogh called *'enlightened
Keynesian economic policy'* was carried to very considerable lengths
in Britain – in marked contrast with the German Federal Republic.
Certainly Lord Balogh, Lord Kaldor, and Lord Kahn could enjoy
the full satisfaction of knowing how amply their grave warnings

---

[1] *Germany: An Experiment in 'Planning' by the 'Free' Price Mechanism*, Blackwell,
1950, p. 7. Though he has been quite prepared, when it has suited him, to invoke
the magic name of Keynes for polemical purposes, Lord Balogh should not, of
course, be described as 'Keynesian', or 'neo-Keynesian'. In fact, Lord Balogh has
rightly insisted that the 'revolution' was 'never fully accepted by Keynes', who
later became an advocate of 'what really amounts to . . . something like *laissez-
faire*'. In other words, in Joan Robinson's terms, Keynes was 'a bastard Keynesian'.
(v. *Keynes and International Monetary Relations*, A. P. Thirlwall (ed.), *op. cit.*, p. 66.) It
is surely a reasonable speculation that Keynes, had he lived, would have approved
enthusiastically of Dr Erhardt's policies and there are few, or no, grounds for
supposing that he would have condemned them. Incidentally, by the later 1970s
some Labour party economists were actually trying to claim that Federal Germany's
economic successes were due to *their* kind of policies.

[2] Joan Robinson's Presidential Address to Section F of the British Association, 1972,
reprinted in M. Keynes (ed.), *Essays on J. M. Keynes*, *op. cit.*, p. 123; and R. Harrod,
'The Arrested Revolution', *New Statesman*, 5 December, 1969, p. 808.

of the 1950s and 1960s had apparently been heeded by governments in Britain. Nobody in Britain could complain that they had been led astray by the 'obsolete' and 'iniquitous' system which Dr Erhardt – flouting 'enlightened *Keynesian* economic policy' – had launched in the German Federal Republic. Nobody in Britain could complain that the 'weakness' of trade unions had inhibited the increase of productivity – as in the German Federal Republic. Surely, as regards the perilous 'dangers of a régime of stable prices', it could justly be claimed that governments in Britain had come to avoid them like the plague. Certainly, again, through all the vagaries of 'wages policies', the 'economic expediency' of abandoning 'any idea of the stability of the price-level' has been meticulously respected.

The very familiar closing words of Keynes's *General Theory* may well exaggerate somewhat the influence of the ideas of economists.[1] But if, in practice, economic doctrines have exercised *any* influence on the course of economic policies between, say, 1946 and 1976, the doctrines of Pseudo-Keynesian economics would seem in Britain to have been more influential than any others.[2]

In 1967 Sir Austin Robinson proclaimed:

'I think we can honestly say that the world today is a different place from what it was in the 1930s in very large measure as a result of the economic thinking that began in this Faculty in Cambridge in those exciting years of the 1930s.'[3]

This is a rather spacious claim. If we may leave the world as a whole out of account, we might presume, however, that this

---

[1] 'The ideas of economists and political philosophers, both when they are right and when they are wrong, are more powerful than is commonly understood. Indeed the world is ruled by little else. Practical men, who believe themselves to be quite exempt from any intellectual influence, are usually the slaves of some defunct economist. Madmen in authority, who hear voices in the air, are distilling their frenzy from some academic scribbler of a few years back.' (*The General Theory of Employment, Interest and Money*, Macmillan, 1936, p. 383.) In recent history surely no more valid (or less invalid) illustration of Keynes's assertions could be found than the dash for growth of 1971-73 'distilled' from the fashionable academic growthmanship of 10-15 years previously.

[2] 'The key point to note is that eighteen years ago three of the greatest Keynesians offered their countrymen monetary expansion, indifference to inflation, and the irrelevance of deficits.' (W. Eltis, 'The Failure of the Keynesian Conventional Wisdom', *Lloyds Bank Review*, October 1976, p. 18.) We would add that this 'Keynesian conventional wisdom' had little basis in, or affinity with, the writings of Keynes.

[3] *Economic Planning in the United Kingdom*, CUP, 1967.

claim might also be thought to have some validity for Britain's position in the 'exciting years' of the 1970s.

The divergence between Keynes and the Pseudo-Keynesians

We would emphasise, however, that we are not here primarily concerned with the question as to *how far* 'Neo-' or Pseudo-Keynesian doctrines actually influenced British economic policy, nor with the question whether such effects as they did have – if any – were beneficial, or catastrophically damaging for the British economy and for the morale and standards of living of the British people. *We are mainly and primarily concerned with an episode in the history of economic thought, that is, with the change and contrast between the views expressed by Keynes on employment targets and inflation, and the views propagated in his name by his self-styled followers in the 1950s and 1960s.* Professor Moggridge who, as editor of the Keynes papers, has something of the role of an official spokesman, has written:

> 'It is clear . . . from Keynes's war-time discussions of the implications of working the economy at "full employment" that he, for one, had before his death not come to any firm policy conclusions.'[1]

But, as we have seen, *Lord Kahn, Sir Roy Harrod, Joan Robinson, Lord Balogh and others (not including Lord Kaldor) were repeatedly proclaiming, in the 'fifties and 'sixties, what the 'Keynesian', or 'Neo-Keynesian' views were, or what Keynes would have been advocating, decades after his death, regarding the problems of the day* – which, oddly enough, usually turned out to coincide precisely with their own particular nostrums, and to diverge very widely from what Keynes had said in some of his latest relevant writings. Only belatedly, in the 'seventies, when the problems of the British economy had indeed become baffling, were Lord Kahn and Sir Roy Harrod sometimes to be found dismissing as 'a nonsense question' what Keynes would be advocating today, to which it would be 'most inappropriate' for them to provide an answer.[2] We would agree with Mr Tim Congdon's conclusion:

---

[1] *Encounter*, September 1975, p. 89; also my letter in *Encounter*, March 1977, p. 92.
[2] *On Re-reading Keynes, op. cit.,* p. 33; and D. Moggridge (ed.), *op. cit.,* p. 8, where Sir Roy Harrod inquired regarding the problem of inflation in the 1970s: 'What do we do? What is the remedy? It would be most inappropriate for me to stand up here and tell you what Keynes would have thought.' But in the 1970s, as we have

[*Contd. on page 37*]

'It is important, therefore, to examine carefully the credentials of any group which calls itself "Keynesian". . . . The Keynesians . . . have freedom to propound their own views as those of Keynes – and it amounts to a licence to counterfeit his intellectual coinage. . . .

They have propagated an influential, but spurious, oral tradition.'[1]

[Contd. from page 36]

seen, Sir Roy knew 'certainly', and had 'no doubt at all', about 'what Keynes would have thought' – at least when this coincided with Sir Roy's ideas. Again, as late as 13 January, 1977, Sir Roy was proclaiming in a letter to *The Times,* 'how furious Keynes, joint founder of the IMF, would have been' at the conditions under which Britain was borrowing; although the rate of inflation and the magnitudes of the external payments, and budgetary, deficits were at levels unprecedented in peacetime.

[1] Congdon, 'Are We Really All Keynesians Now?', *op. cit.,* pp. 23-24.

VIII. Economists and Inflation

Regarding economists generally in the 'fifties and 'sixties, Dr Gunnar Myrdal has complained of their

> 'slowness to recognise what had become and was to remain the main post-war problem, namely inflation. . . . Few economists made an early move to analyse the problem in any depth. Some of them even invented reasons why a measure of inflation was needed to speed up economic growth and stabilise economic development. Practically nobody tried seriously to spell out the thesis . . . that inflation has arbitrary, unintended and therefore undesirable effects on resource allocation and the distribution of incomes and wealth.'[1]

Sir Dennis Robertson's critique . . .
One may certainly doubt whether Dr Myrdal's accusations would ever have been valid against Keynes himself, had he lived. But they obviously apply to the prevailing Pseudo-Keynesian body of opinion in Britain, where inflation, since the early 1950s, had remained, for the most part, more serious than in most other similar countries. Outstanding among those economists in Britain who warned against the dangers of inflation in the 'fifties had been Sir Dennis Robertson, who had generally supported Keynes's policy proposals in the inter-war years and who emphasised (1955):

> '. . . both the admitted inequities and the long-term economic and social dangers generated by even a slow inflationary process are so apparent that some of those who accept it as inevitable, and even on balance desirable, have felt moved to make suggestions for modifying the incidence of its impact.'

But, as Sir Dennis went on to point out, regarding attempts at 'modifying the incidence' of inflation at an earlier, not intolerable stage:

> 'The rush for the band-wagon would set the wagon itself smartly rolling forward, and there would always be somebody left lagging

---

[1] *Against the Stream: Critical Essays on Economics*, Macmillan, 1973, pp. 19-21.

behind. But what that means is that the planned orderly fall in the value of money would be in danger of turning into a landslide, generating not a comfortable condition of "full employment" but a hectic and disorderly muddle, which could only be checked, at the cost of much disemployment and distress, by the re-establishment of drastic monetary discipline.'[1]

But then, Sir Dennis was an outmoded, 'neo-classical' economist.

. . . and Lord Robbins's warnings

Alongside those of Sir Dennis Robertson, the warnings of Lord Robbins should be cited, as imparted particularly in his paper, 'Full Employment as an Objective' (1949).[2] Together with the dangers of inflation and economic authoritarianism, Lord Robbins emphasised the implications of an open-ended commitment by government to the trade unions to the effect that 'whatever rate of wages you call for, we are prepared to inflate sufficiently to prevent unemployment'. Lord Robbins concluded:

'To frame policy with an eye *inter alia* to the maintenance of high levels of employment is wisdom. To frame it with regard to full employment *only* is likely to lead to disappointment and even, perhaps, to something worse than disappointment.'

Pseudo-Keynesian abandonment of Keynes's caution

On the other hand, Pseudo-Keynesian doctrines followed the tastes of public and politicians in abandoning the caution and moderation evident in Keynes's own writings, and in far-reachingly neglecting the dangers and injustices of inflation and probable losses of freedom; unlike Keynes who, on the one peace-time occasion (1920) when an outburst of inflation threatened the British economy during his life-time, proposed thoroughly drastic measures.[3] There are no grounds for arguing that Keynes would have abandoned

---

[1] *Essays in Money and Interest*, Collins/Fontana Library, 1966, pp. 251-2.

[2] Reprinted in Robbins, *The Economist in the Twentieth Century*, Macmillan, 1954, pp. 18-40. We might add, however, that we are certainly not among those who would suggest that Lord Robbins should, in the 'seventies, retract his retraction (made in the late 'thirties and 'forties) of his fundamental opposition to the public works policies of Keynes and the majority of English economists in the early 'thirties. (Peter Jay, *The Times*, 17 February, 1977, p. 19.)

[3] v. S. Howson, 'A Dear Money Man? Keynes on Monetary Policy 1920', *Economic Journal*, June 1973, pp. 456ff; and Tim Congdon, 'Are We Really All Keynesians Now?', *op. cit.*, pp. 23 ff.

his previous caution, or employment targets, because of pressure from, or unpopularity with, politicians and public.[1] In fact, there are no valid grounds for assuming that in the 'fifties Keynes would have *dis*agreed with Sir Dennis Robertson and Lord Robbins, rather than with Lord Kahn, Joan Robinson and Sir Roy Harrod.

It is important to emphasise the connection between inflation and government intervention in and regulation of the economy. Although Pseudo-Keynesian economists did not, of course, *want* inflation, some of them – *quite unlike Keynes* – wanted very much indeed its usual fruits and consequences in the form of wage- and price-controls, regulation of profits, widespread subsidisation, import-controls, etc., for which inflation provides a pretext. Some of the more extreme Pseudo-Keynesians were certainly strongly in favour of destroying the mixed economy and replacing it by a régime of 'purposive direction' and 'comprehensive planning'. A permissive attitude to the money supply is well calculated to promote such objectives, and sophisticated defences for such permissiveness were devised.[2]

---

[1] We do not agree with all Professor Hayek's judgements on Keynes, but the following seems completely convincing: 'I have little doubt that we owe much of the post-war inflation to the great influence of such over-simplified Keynesianism. Not that Keynes himself would have approved of this. Indeed, I am fairly certain that if he had lived he would in that period have been one of the most determined fighters against inflation. About the last time I saw him, a few weeks before his death, he more or less plainly told me so. As his remark on that occasion is illuminating in other respects, it is worth reporting. I had asked him whether he was not getting alarmed about the use to which some of his disciples were putting his theories. His reply was that these theories had been greatly needed in the 1930s, but if these theories should ever become harmful, I could be assured that he would quickly bring about a change in public opinion.' (*A Tiger by the Tail*, Hobart Paperback 4, IEA, 1972, 2nd edn., 1978, p. 103.)

[2] It was not that the deliberate and explicit wrecking of the mixed economy by the encouragement of inflation was propagated by all Pseudo-Keynesians in the name of Keynes. However, such a policy was explicitly advocated by two Oxford economists, Messrs A. Glyn and B. Sutcliffe, who claimed: 'We have shown that capitalism will be unable to continue accepting the rate of wage increase which has prevailed in the recent past without jeopardising its own existence.' The controversial normative or political message was then proclaimed: 'This means that the working-class leaders must adopt a new attitude to wage demands: they must realise that wage claims are becoming political weapons in a battle in which the existence of capitalism is at stake. *By abolishing the private ownership of capital and redistributing income a socialist system could almost immediately provide a decent standard of life for everyone.*' However, unlike Joan Robinson and others, Messrs Glyn and Sutcliffe did not describe their views as 'neo-' or 'post-Keynesian'. (*British Capitalism, Workers and the Profits Squeeze*, Penguin Books, 1972, pp. 10, 202 and 215; italics added.)

Those ready to take risks with inflation were certainly not unprepared for, and indeed strongly in favour of, comprehensive government intervention, even, in some cases, in accordance with the Soviet model.[1] In fact, what might be described as 'Pseudo-Keynesian' economics consisted, to a large extent, of urging politicians on to over-full employment and growthmanship, while claiming that the latest Wage Restraint or Prices and Incomes Policy, Statement of Intent, or the Planned Growth of Incomes, or Social Compact or Contract, etc., etc., etc., not merely *might eventually* restrain (it was nice to believe) but *was already* restraining and keeping inflation down to a harmless level – all accompanied by constant invocations of the magic name of Keynes.[2]

There can be no doubt that Pseudo-Keynesian economists in Britain rejected what Keynes advocated as the

'attempt to use what we have learnt from modern experience and modern analysis, not to defeat, but to implement the wisdom of Adam Smith.'

In practice, Pseudo-Keynesian economics amounted to a wholesale rejection, in the domestic field, of that kind of 'classical medicine' of which Keynes wrote at the end of his last article (1946):

'If we reject the medicine from our systems altogether, we may just drift on from expedient to expedient and never get really fit again.'[3]

---

[1] 'I am confident that in the end we shall find that full employment can be obtained only by aiming high, and if the investment target is over-shot, by controlling cumulative movements directly and by fiscal measures. This was the way the Soviet obtained its results and I doubt whether we can do better.' (Lord Balogh, *Planning for Progress*, Fabian Society, 1963, p. 23.)

[2] For example, as early as 1956 Sir Roy Harrod was claiming: 'Some hold that wage-earners are greedy, not to say insatiable, and that, with full-employment, they will persistently bid up their wage demands more than the rise in productivity and that we are thereby doomed to a régime of chronic inflation. I regard this as unduly pessimistic.' (*Time and Tide*, 28 July, 1956, p. 900.) In 1958, as we have noticed, Lord Kahn was referring to the 'considerable improvements in the state of awareness of the importance of restraint over wage increases'. Lord Balogh, after proclaiming in 1964 that 'the greater equality implied by tax reform will provide the basis for a national incomes policy', was announcing that the Labour Government had 'obtained support of the trade unions for a well-conceived plan for an incomes policy'. (v. *Economics and Economic Policy* . . ., *op. cit.*, p. 225.)

[3] *Economic Journal, op. cit.*, p. 186.

IX. Keynes and
'the Keynesian Revolution'

We have not been concerned here with basic criticisms of Keynes's more 'general' theories, or of the more general aspects of his theories, which are not subject to the kind of obsolescence, or irrelevance, due to historical and institutional change. In this field, shelves-full of literature have long existed. We are, however, to some extent, though not primarily, concerned with the extent to which Keynes's doctrines were based on empirical propositions or assumptions, for which there may have been much justification in his own day, but which have been rendered seriously invalid or irrelevant by historical and institutional changes. This is a kind of obsolescence, or source of anomaly, to which theories in economics are seriously liable, and which is sometimes not recognised, or sufficiently allowed for, by economists who over-confidently assume a kind of epistemological parity with the natural sciences.

Keynes's basic assumptions obsolete

It is obvious enough, to start with, that whereas Keynes's *General Theory* assumed deflation, stagnation, and heavy unemployment, within about four years of its publication inflation and very high levels of employment had generally become, and have since remained, the rule. Much more specifically, both Mr Colin Clark and Professor Milton Friedman, for example, have emphasised (from contrasting points of view) the obsolescence of Keynes's basic assumption about money and real wages and the 'money illusion' of workers.[1] Another major contrast between the conditions of

---

[1] Mr Clark emphasises that the assumption of workers' money illusion 'was an important but purely temporary truth from the 1930s', and that 'even as a theory only valid for a short period, in a time of heavy unemployment, the doctrine of labour's "money illusion" was applicable only in the advanced industrial countries.' (*Taxmanship*, Hobart Paper 26, 2nd edn., IEA, 1970, pp. 54-5.) Milton Friedman also questioned more fundamentally the 'money illusion' assumption: *Unemployment versus Inflation*, Occasional Paper 44, IEA, 1975, p. 17. Mr Walter Eltis suggests two further institutional changes in the role of the British economy which
[*Contd. on page 43*]

the 'thirties and those of the post-war British economy has been emphasised by Professor R. C. O. Matthews, that is, what he calls 'the trend increase in the scarcity of labour relative to capital'.[1]

Fundamental alterations to Keynes's doctrines

However, our primary concern here is not with this kind of historical or institutional obsolescence, to which virtually all empirically significant economic theories may be more or less liable. We are concerned primarily with the distortion or alteration of Keynes's tentative policy-doctrines and objectives, and with the unjustifiable invocation of his name on behalf of doctrines which there are no good grounds for supposing he would have supported.

It should be emphasised that the alterations to Keynes's doctrines did not amount simply to normative changes in policy-preferences, or in

---

[*Contd. from page 42*]
have undermined the relevance or feasibility of Keynes's doctrines.

First, relatively smaller economies cannot pursue Keynesian methods of raising employment as can more powerful countries: '. . . it is the great and powerful that must follow Keynesian deficit-financing policies. It is they whom Keynes addressed in 1936 (when he addressed the powerful by addressing his own country-men). . . . But the weaknesses in these policies have not been understood, so small countries like Britain in the 1960s and 1970s, advised by Keynesian fine-tuners, have accelerated domestic inflation and destroyed the international values of their currencies, either deliberately or accidentally, under the mistaken belief that they were pursuing full employment.' At this point we may note the contrast with Mr H. D. Henderson in 1933 insisting: 'World recovery can indeed only be brought about if the stronger financial countries lead the way and we belong to this category.' (S. Howson and D. Winch, *The Economic Advisory Council 1930-1939*, *op. cit.*, p. 129.)

Secondly, Mr Eltis maintains, regarding the rate of interest and international complications: 'Keynes's assumptions that the British interest rate is independent of foreign interest rates and that government bonds are a typical portfolio asset are comprehensible in the context of the Britain of the 1930s. London was then a great financial centre, so if he believed that world interest rates were determined in London, with sterling the *numéraire* against which other currencies were at a premium or discount, this would not have been absurd. . . . in 1936 it might have been reasonable to regard bonds as a typical portfolio asset.' (The two quotations from Mr Eltis are from his trenchant article, 'The Failure of the Keynesian Conventional Wisdom', *Lloyds Bank Review*, October 1976, pp. 8 and 12.)

[1] *Economic Journal*, September 1968, p. 568. Professor Matthews observes: 'When the question is asked, *why* have we had full employment since the war?, most people tend to reply, without thinking very much, that it is because we have had a full-employment policy – we have had the Keynesian revolution. Now supposing this were the right answer, it would be a remarkable thing. It would mean that the most important single feature of the post-war British economy has been due to an advance in economic theory. It would be a most striking vindication of Keynes's celebrated dictum about the ultimate primacy of abstract thought in the world of affairs. However, this interpretation of events, at least in its simple form, is open to serious objections' (p. 556).

objectives, or values, regarding the trade-off between unemployment and inflation. The alterations we have cited amounted to a fundamental change in positive theory, regarding how the economy worked. Keynes, in 1937, was ready to step up public investment or public works to bring down unemployment to somewhere in the region of 10-12 per cent. He then pointed to the 'rigidity' of the British economy, which necessitated what he called 'a different technique' from that of 'a further general stimulus at the centre' by additional government spending. Of course Keynes *might*, quite possibly or probably, have revised what seemed subsequently a high estimate of the natural rate, or the level of unemployment at which to break off the stimulus to aggregate demand by increased central government spending. But he clearly thought that there was some *quite significant* level of unemployment at which the policy of stimulating general government spending should be curbed. Therefore, what Professor David Laidler maintains about 'Keynesian' economics may unfortunately be true enough; but it is not true about the writings of Keynes (with which, of course, 'Keynesian economics' has had only incidental similarities):

> '*The whole intellectual basis of post-war "demand management" by government is undermined if the natural unemployment rate hypothesis is true.* Policy is based on the assumption that Keynesian economics tells us how we may attain *any* level of unemployment we think desirable simply by manipulating monetary and fiscal policy.'[1]

Keynes and the natural rate hypothesis

Keynes's most relevant writings showed that he at least strongly suspected that something like what Professor Laidler calls 'the natural rate hypothesis' *was true in 1937 – the last fully peace-time year Keynes experienced.* Keynes himself clearly did *not* 'tell us how [or that] we may attain *any* level of unemployment we think desirable simply by manipulating monetary and fiscal policy'.

It must be remembered that the unemployment problem in Britain, and the intensive study of it, did not begin with Keynes, but well before the First World War. It was in 1905, for example, that Joseph Chamberlain proclaimed:

---

[1] David Laidler, 'The End of "Demand Management": How to Reduce Unemployment in the 1970s', a British Commentary to Milton Friedman's *Unemployment versus Inflation?*, Occasional Paper 44, IEA, 1975, p. 45 (italics in original).

'The question of employment, believe me, has now become the most important question of our time.'[1]

The pioneer works appeared in the decade before the war with the contributions of Beveridge, Pigou, and the Royal Commission on the Poor Laws. Before the emergence and dominance of the Keynesian theory of deficiencies in aggregate effective demand, the analysis of unemployment was in terms of its different types – frictional, seasonal, cyclical, etc. Policy proposals were in terms of specific measures appropriate to these different types, and can be said, to a significant or large extent, to have consisted of measures designed to reduce the 'natural rate'. This was most obviously the case with measures to reduce 'frictional' unemployment by creating labour exchanges (as carried out by Churchill, with Beveridge as his *aide,* before World War I). Keynes was well aware of these differing types of unemployment even if 'Keynesians' were, or are, not. But his own main contribution was directed to the extremely high levels of unemployment in the inter-war years which seem to have been persistently above the natural rate, however precisely defined (as were, possibly or probably, also the levels reached in the deeper depressions of the 19th-century business cycle).

As Mr Colin Clark has observed:

'Even now we are still standing too close to make a real assessment of Keynes's contributions to economics, how far they represented permanent additions to our methods of analysis, to what extent they were *ad hoc* proposals to put right the tragic and unnecessary unemployment and depression of the 1930s, *which would have been valuable if applied at the time but which may have become irrelevant or positively misleading later.*'[2]

Keynes's proposals in the 1930s for reducing unemployment had a specially important role for fiscal policy and public works – though we have seen that he stated clearly that 'public loan expenditure' was '*not necessarily the best way to increase employment*'. By the time of Keynes's death the nature and magnitude of the unemployment problem had obviously begun to change fundamentally from what it had been in the 'thirties. Whatever precise role for 'demand management' remained, or, in particular, for 'the general stimulus at the centre', by public loan expenditure, of aggregate demand, a

---

[1] R. Skidelsky, *New Statesman,* 22 October, 1976, p. 542.

[2] *Taxmanship, op. cit.,* p. 53 (italics added).

relatively much more important role emerged for the 'different technique' which, in 1937, Keynes had called for in view of the 'unfortunately rigid' structure of the British economy. It seems clear that this 'different technique' to deal with rigidity would have broadly corresponded, in *some* important respects, with the kind of proposals to reduce 'frictional' and other forms of unemployment put forward by the pre-Keynesian pioneers before 1914. It seems equally clear that Keynes's 'different technique' would also have broadly corresponded, in *some* important respects, with what today, following Professor Friedman, is described as reducing the natural rate of unemployment.

Pseudo-Keynesians have not recognised the various and changing aspects of the unemployment problem and thereby have propagated different policies and objectives from those of Keynes himself. But it would be quite unjust, especially in view of his explicit and open-minded recognition of the different types and aspects of unemployment and the different policies it requires, to attribute any kind of dogmatic blindness, or *mystique*, to Keynes. However, the Pseudo-Keynesians have certainly supplied an excellent example for Professor Bronfenbrenner's general account (quoted in Chapter I, page 2) of how it may come about that a once-triumphant theory, 'thesis', or 'paradigm' 'hardens from doctrine to dogma', and how

'. . . the thesis turns apologetic, repetitive, and lifeless . . . because problems arise for which the answers stemming from orthodox paradigms are either lacking or unacceptable.'

But just as mistaken as a failure to recognise its subsequent decline would be a denial of the original achievements of the 'revolution' in, and for, its own time.

Towards a more accurate record of the history of economics
Our main and primary concern in this *Paper* has been with the history of economic thought, that is, with contributing to the formation of a less inaccurate record, which is an important task from the point of view of intellectual standards, and also one not devoid of practical and political significance. We are also concerned with the clarification of the extent and limits of knowledge and ignorance in economics. In its heyday 'the Keynesian revolution' helped to build up generally over-optimistic notions about economic

knowledge, and more specifically about how far methods had been discovered for maintaining any desired levels of employment at negligible cost with the support of incomes policies; while simultaneously, and on top of that, it was suggested that 'purposive' neo-Keynesian growth policies would (about) double British rates of growth. In fact, 'the Keynesian revolution' was carried far beyond anything contemplated in the writings of Keynes. Disillusion has been politically dangerous. Though unfortunately belated, it is surely better late than never to attempt to disperse illusions and seek to attain a less inaccurate and more realistic grasp of the extent and limits of economic knowledge.[1]

---

[1] I have discussed this subject more fully in *Knowledge and Ignorance in Economics*, Blackwell, 1977.

CRITIQUES OF THE GENERAL ARGUMENT

A Comment

by

LORD KAHN

Professor of Economics, University of Cambridge, 1951-72
Fellow of King's College, Cambridge

Professor Hutchison has been assiduous in tracking down quotations from economists covering a wide range of beliefs. I am reminded of Dennis Robertson's remark in a controversy with Keynes, that it is most unlikely to be helpful to clap a particular

> 'label *opprobrii causa* on to the vacuous countenance of some composite Aunt Sally of uncertain age.'[1]

To quote Professor Donald Moggridge,

> 'one can find more than enough ammunition in Keynes for many varied points of view, especially if . . . [one] wishes to lift it out of context.'[2]

'How to Avoid a Slump'

I begin with the importance attached by Professor Hutchison to the three articles by Keynes on 'How to Avoid a Slump', published in *The Times* in January 1937.[3] The number of unemployed was $1\frac{3}{4}$ million, a percentage of 12 per cent. Professor Hutchison explains that Keynes did not regard 12 per cent unemployment as the minimum to be aimed at but that what was needed was a rightly distributed demand rather than a larger aggregate.

I attach more importance than, I think, does Professor Hutchison to Keynes's speech[4] of 25 February, 1937, and to his article in *The Times* of 11 March.[5] By then the Government had announced a programme of accelerated rearmament, to be financed by borrowing. The final passage quoted by Professor Hutchison from the article indicates that Keynes regarded an unemployment

---

[1] *Economic Journal*, September 1937, p. 436.

[2] Donald Moggridge, in a letter commenting on an article by Mr Tim Congdon, *Encounter*, September 1975, p. 89.

[3] Pp. 10 to 12 above, and Appendix A, pp. 65-73.

[4] Delivered as Chairman of the National Mutual Life Assurance Company, p. 12 above.

[5] Pp. 12-13 above, and Appendix B, pp. 74-77.

percentage of somewhat above 6 per cent as 'safe', though perhaps 'rather near the limit'.

Professor Hutchison does not quote Keynes's statement that 'careful planning and an interval for the planning to take effect' would ease the problem, as would 'transfer of labour' and 'measures to ensure that all possible orders are placed in the Special Areas where surplus resources are available'.

Of considerable importance is Keynes's answer, given in the same article, to the question 'What do we mean by "inflation"?':

> 'If we mean by the term a state of affairs which is dangerous and ought to be avoided – and, since the term carries to most people an opprobrious implication, this is the convenient usage – then we must not mean by it merely that prices and wages are rising. For a rising tendency of prices and wages inevitably, and for obvious reasons, accompanies any revival of activity. ... It is when increased demand is no longer capable of materially raising output and employment and mainly spends itself in raising prices that it is properly called inflation. When this point is reached, the new demand merely competes with the existing demand for the use of resources which are already employed to the utmost.'

There seems to me to be no justification for Professor Hutchison's statement that 'in 1937 Keynes was clearly concerned with the possible dangers of inflation when unemployment was still around 11 to 12 per cent'.[1] A figure of 6 to 7 per cent seems to be justified. The difference between these two orders of magnitude is highly significant.

Rearmament controversy

The ironic comments[2] of Professor Hutchison on an article of mine indicate that he is unaware of the terrible controversy which was raging in the second half of the 1930s about the speed of rearmament. Keynes was passionately in favour of acceleration. Knowing in January 1937 that there was a good chance that the Government would shortly take an important step, he felt that it was tactically wise to make only a passing reference to rearmament and to reserve his economic analysis until after the Government had published their plans late in February.

---

[1] Page 14 above.
[2] Pp. 17-20 above.

The Government were afraid that rearmament would interfere with the normal course of trade. Keynes was anxious to relieve them of this anxiety for as long as possible. That is why he did not advocate 'public works' and the like to reduce unemployment. He wanted the 'public works' to take the form of expenditure on arms growing as rapidly as possible. By the beginning of 1940, four months after the outbreak of the war, unemployment had risen to two million. Keynes was in a strong position to ridicule the Government for sluggishness.

In May 1939 Keynes gave a talk on the BBC.[1] Unemployment, in spite of expenditure on rearmament, was still about $1\frac{1}{2}$ million. Keynes predicted that

> 'as compared with last year, the number of unemployed should fall in the course of the year by 500,000 as a minimum. And some people think that a good case can be made out for putting the estimate half as big again as this, or even double.'

On top of this would be the effect of recruitment by the Armed Forces. (It is not clear for what period of time Keynes made this prediction. But although the number of unemployed was slightly over $1\frac{1}{2}$ million in January 1940, by May the number had fallen to 800,000.)

In the course of this talk, Keynes said:

> 'What a difference all this makes. It is not an exaggeration to say that the end of abnormal unemployment is in sight . . .'
>
> 'I have a special reason for hoping that trade unionists will do what they can to make this transition to fuller employment work smoothly. I began by saying that the grand experiment has begun. If it works, if expenditure on armaments really does cure unemployment, I predict that we shall never go all the way back to the old state of affairs. If we can cure unemployment for the purpose of armaments, we can cure it for the productive purpose of peace. Good may come out of evil. We may learn a trick or two which will come in useful when the day of peace comes, as in the fullness of time it must.'

This is a radically different Keynes from the one depicted by Professor Hutchison. The appeal to trade unionists is significant. What Keynes was afraid of is indicated by the reply by the TUC in December 1939, *after* the war had broken out, to an appeal for

---

[1] *The Listener*, 1 June, 1939.

restraint on the wages front from Sir John Simon, the Chancellor of the Exchequer:

> 'No, Sir John, we cannot agree with your suggestion for a truce in wage increases, mainly because each union preserves its autonomy to apply for its own increases.'[1]

On 'How to Pay for the War' and wartime policy

Keynes did not begin to work in the Treasury until June 1940, but he had published his booklet on *How to Pay for the War*.[2] In it he advocated, *inter alia*, a constant price-level, secured by subsidies, and an agreement on the part of trade unions, if this price-level did not rise, not to press for an increase of wages.

> 'For the trade unions such a scheme as this offers great and evident advantages compared with progressive inflation. . . . We should have succeeded in making the war an opportunity for a positive social improvement. How great a benefit in comparison with a futile attempt to evade a reasonable share of the burden of a just war, ending in a progressive inflation!'

Keynes's proposals were accepted only in part. During the course of the war the wage-rate index rose by 49·2 per cent and the cost of living by 31·6 per cent – average annual rates of about 8 and 6 per cent.

Professor Hutchison mentions that 'During the war, when unemployment had been reduced to below 1 per cent, Keynes was apparently prepared to suggest about $4\frac{1}{2}$ per cent unemployment as an equilibrium level for peace-time. But he was sceptical about the feasibility of the Beveridge target of 3 per cent.'[3]

Beveridge's 3 per cent was an average, not a minimum, and was arrived at 'as a conservative, rather than an unduly hopeful, aim to set'. In December 1944 Keynes wrote to Beveridge warmly congratulating him on his book, and adding in a postscript:

> 'No harm in aiming at 3 per cent unemployed, but I shall be surprised if we succeed.'

---

[1] *Daily Express*, 12 December, 1939.

[2] Originally in the form of two articles in *The Times*, 14 and 15 November, 1939; in an enlarged form in February 1940: *The Collected Writings of John Maynard Keynes*, Macmillan for the Royal Economic Society, Vol. IX: *Essays in Persuasion*, pp. 367–439.

[3] Page 15 above.

The significant words are 'No harm'. To me they indicate awareness of the political and administrative problems rather than any fear of the economic consequence of the level of unemployment falling, at times, below 3 per cent. My two preceding paragraphs suggest that Keynes's ideas about the safe minimum level had changed radically since January 1937.

Wages, prices, unemployment and the unions

While Keynes did not have time, before his premature death, to work out any systematic theory of the behaviour of wages and prices at low levels of unemployment, there are various indications that he did not believe in any mechanical relationship between the behaviour of wages and prices and the level of unemployment. He regarded the problem as 'essentially political'. In a letter[1] written in December 1943 Keynes asked:

> 'How much otherwise avoidable unemployment do you propose to bring about in order to keep the Trade Unions in order? Do you think that it will be politically possible when they understand what you are up to? My own preliminary view is that other, more reasonable, less punitive measures must be found.'

In another letter[2] of the same date he wrote:

> 'If money wages rise faster than efficiency, this aggravates the difficulty of maintaining full employment, and it is one of the main obstacles which a full employment policy has to overcome. . . .
>
> Some people over here are accustomed to argue that the fear of unemployment and the recurrent experience of it are the only means by which, in past practice, Trade Unions have been prevented from over-doing their wage-raising pressure. I hope this is not true. . . . The more aware we were of the risk, the more likely we should be to find a way round other than totalitarianism. But I recognised the reality of this risk. . . . It is a *political* rather than an economic problem.'

Here can be seen the germs – but no more than the germs – of incomes policy, under which the rate of increase in wages and prices is largely determined as a result of negotiations on a political plane.

---

[1] Keynes Papers, not yet published.
[2] *Ibid.*

'Natural rate of unemployment'

Professor Hutchison is foolish to talk about the 'natural rate of unemployment', and still more foolish to state that 'Keynes may be said to have suggested a similar concept', though not 'as clearly as it came to be understood in the 'seventies'.[1]

The level of unemployment does not, according to monetarists, determine the rate of increase in the price-level in the Phillips sense. It determines – according to whether it is above or below the natural rate – whether the rate of inflation is decelerating or accelerating. If unemployment is at the natural level, the rate of inflation is constant. But it can be high or low, being determined by the rate of increase in the quantity of money.

Professor Hutchison states that 'Unemployment in Britain, between 1921 and 1939, seems almost continuously to have been above anything describable as the natural level'.[2] I am doubtful whether he means more than that measures designed to reduce unemployment were desirable, and would not result in inflation. But if he believes in the modern monetarist concept of the 'natural rate', he has to explain why, in the two decades before the war, the price-level did not fall faster and faster.[3]

The estimates which have been made by monetarists for the natural rate of unemployment in Britain are entirely inconsistent with Professor Hutchison's percentages of 11 to 12 per cent, or even, if he makes the concession I request,[4] 6 to 7 per cent, based on Keynes's pre-war articles – if he really thinks they represent the natural rate.

'What the natural rate of unemployment might be would be extremely hard to assess: preliminary results of work in progress at Manchester University suggest that it is perhaps a little less than 2 per cent in Britain . . .'

I quote Professor David Laidler.[5] More recent work suggests that it

---

[1] Pp. 14-15 above.

[2] Page 6 above.

[3] Francis Cripps, 'The money supply, wages and inflation', *Cambridge Journal of Economics*, Vol. I, No. 1, March 1977, p. 105.

[4] Pp. 14-15 and 48-49 above.

[5] David Laidler in *Unemployment versus Inflation?*, Occasional Paper 44, IEA, 1975, p. 45.

'must have risen very considerably since the mid-1960s – from under 2 per cent to nearly 4 per cent.'[1]

In commenting on the applicability of Keynes's teaching to the period following the end of the war, Professor Hutchison is wrong in referring to a doctrine of 'expanding aggregate demand'. Though to a far lesser extent than in the war, it was British Government policy – and indeed still is – to curtail the pressure of demand. Needs were – and still are – far greater than the available productive potential could cope with.[2] Under these conditions, Keynesian policy means restricting, not expanding, demand. Professor Hutchison ignores the Keynes of *How to Pay for the War*, and his work in the Treasury.

One of my criticisms of the management of the economy since the war is that government restraints have fallen too much on productive investment as opposed to consumption, both personal and public.[3] During considerable parts of the period the restraints, usually as a result of an adverse balance-of-payments position, have resulted in recessions, which, although not, until recently, very great, have discouraged industrialists from carrying out their investment plans. This is one of the reasons for our low rate of growth of productivity.

Professor Hutchison describes me in 1956 as simply proclaiming 'the Beveridge target of 3 per cent as "obsolete" '.[4] What I wrote was:

'The growth of productivity depends very largely on securing a high level of physical investment. That is why it seems so important to find a means of reconciling high rates of investment and employment with an acceptable behaviour of the money-wage level and to avoid being driven into a policy involving really effective restraints on investment

---

[1] Cripps, *loc. cit.*, p. 107, based on a paper written in Manchester University in 1975 by M. R. Gray, J. M. Parkin and M. T. Sumner.

[2] Professor Robin Matthews, 'Why has Britain had Full Employment since the War?', *Economic Journal*, September 1968, p. 556.

[3] Professor Matthews refers to 'high post-war investment', but he explains that he is concerned with the question 'why investment has been so much higher relatively to national income than it has ever been before in this country', although it 'has been low compared with other countries'. (*loc. cit.*, p. 560.) In other words, the inter-war period is a poor base for the purpose of comparison.

[4] Page 27 above.

designed perhaps to bring the ratios of unemployment closer to Lord Beveridge's obsolete 3 per cent.'[1]

I was writing in 1956. The unemployment percentage was only 1·1 per cent. This was largely the result of a substantial rise in the level of industrial investment. On wages and prices the Government had successfully appealed for restraint. In 1957 the average level of wage-rates was 5 per cent higher than in 1956; the average level of retail prices 3 per cent higher. These figures indicate a considerable success for a policy of wage and price restraint.

Evidence to Radcliffe Committee (1958)

Professor Hutchison comments on my written evidence, prepared in 1958, to the Radcliffe Committee.[2] I was at fault in suggesting that wages policy would make it possible to achieve 'stability of the price-level', if the word stability is interpreted literally. But that is not the point at issue. The point which I was making was that:

'If reliance is placed on regulation of demand in order to secure a tolerable behaviour of prices, it must almost certainly mean maintaining unemployment at a level which would represent very serious economic waste as well as political unacceptability.'

As an alternative to restraint of demand I invited the Committee to examine 'the realm of wage negotiation', and consider the desirability of a 'wages policy'.

In my evidence I did state that

'Where creation of slack is most effective in moderating the rise in wages is in respect of what is known as the "wage drift" ... While the behaviour of actual wages is influenced by the course of wage negotiations, they may be bid up by employers under the influence of high demand faster than the negotiated rates.'

I added that

'Apart from periods of marked shortage of labour, I would attribute major responsibility for the upward movement of wages in this country to the competitive struggle between trade unions, and inside some of the trade unions between various sections of labour.'

---

[1] *Selected Essays on Employment and Growth*, C U P, 1972, p. 102.

[2] Page 29 above. A better impression of my argument is, of course, secured by reading the whole of the relevant passages. (*Ibid.*, pp. 137-145.)

The level below which unemployment should not be pushed down depends on the structural character of the economy and on its economic position. The better the provisions for securing mobility of labour – geographical and between skills and trades – the lower is the level to which unemployment can safely be reduced.

Also if the pattern of production is satisfactory, a low level of unemployment can be welcomed. On the other hand, so long as a shift of productive resources is called for – usually into the production of exports and import substitutes and into productive investment – slack is required for a time in order to avoid the shift being held up by labour bottlenecks, provided that measures are taken which will ensure that success is achieved.

I abstract from the unemployment associated with the need to keep down the levels of output and income sufficiently to keep imports low enough to be financed by borrowing from overseas without an unacceptable growth of our overseas debt. I must regretfully add that restraints imposed by the IMF almost certainly result, on top of that, in yet further unemployment.

Mr F. T. Blackaby, of the National Institute of Economic and Social Research, in a paper written early in 1974,[1] has examined the effectiveness of government target rates of unemployment. In the period examined by him, targets varied between $1\frac{1}{2}$ and $2\frac{1}{2}$ per cent, although actual unemployment rose considerably higher in 1971 and 1972. He was mainly concerned with the contention that higher unemployment means a lower rate of price increase.

Mr Blackaby reminds us of Professor F. W. Paish's prediction of 1967, based on the Phillips curve, that the price-level will be constant if the percentage of unemployment is $2\frac{1}{4}$ per cent, or a little less. He feels that 'it is important to remember how much we were promised, and by how many people, from a little rise in unemployment'.[2] Mr Blackaby concludes:

'The economic benefits from the general shift in the target rate of unemployment are not demonstrable, it is doubtful whether there were any. . . . The belief in a beneficial effect from a small change in demand

---

[1] For a conference organised by the Royal Economic Society, reproduced in G. D. N. Worswick (ed.), *The Concept and Measurement of Involuntary Unemployment*, 1976, pp. 279-304.

[2] *Ibid.*, pp. 286 and 287.

pressure, as measured by unemployment, appears to be an Anglo-Saxon idiosyncracy.'

There are some indications of a perverse relation – at certain times and especially at the present time – between the level of unemployment and the rate of inflation.[1] If incomes policy in this country now collapses, with the result that the rate of inflation rises, this can reasonably be attributed, in considerable measure, to the high level of unemployment.

---

[1] See, for example, Ken Coutts, Roger Tarling and Frank Wilkinson, *Economic Policy Review*, Cambridge Department of Applied Economics, No. 1, 1975, No. 2, 1976.

A Comment

by

SIR AUSTIN ROBINSON

Emeritus Professor of Economics, University of Cambridge

Any contribution that I make to this controversy I make with great hesitation. I have no idea by what right and by what criteria Professor Hutchison has assumed the authority to label some of us Keynesians and some of us Pseudo-Keynesians, or why those terms should not be reversed. I have no idea whether in his terminology I personally am a Keynesian or a Pseudo-Keynesian. There have almost from the first been two different meanings attached to 'Keynesian' economics. Keynes's own Cambridge pupils regarded Keynesian economics as being a way of thinking about the factors determining the level of activity, equally applicable to depression and boom. His American disciples have tended to regard Keynesian economics as perpetually expansionary, whatever the current economic climate. I am reminded of Keynes's comment to Lydia[1] and me at breakfast in Washington in 1944 after he had dined the night before with the Washington Keynesian economists: 'I was the only non-Keynesian there.'

I would like to confine myself to the argument about his thinking in 1937-38. To understand this it is necessary to have very clearly in mind that between 1933 and 1937 the economy had expanded by about 23 per cent and the GDP was running about 14 per cent above its earlier maximum in 1929, despite the continuance of about 11 per cent of unemployment. The patterns both of consumption and of investment had greatly changed. Thus many of the features normally associated with full employment – bottle-necks, a rising marginal import-ratio and an adverse current account balance – were manifesting themselves. In these circumstances, as I see it, Keynes took the view that it was for the moment unnecessary and undesirable to give a further impulse to expansion.

A careful reading of his *Times* articles will not, I am convinced, justify the supposition that he regarded 11 per cent or any other

---

[1] [Lydia Lopokova: Lady Keynes. – ED.]

58

rate as a Natural Rate of Unemployment, or as a rate relevant to any but the immediate circumstances. He was primarily concerned with the fact that the economy had now temporarily come up against structural obstacles to further expansion and that structural changes – in particular industrial and infra-structure investment and increased exports – were a necessary prelude to any trouble-free further rapid expansion. These might take time to carry through. Impulse had already been given to industrial investment; it had considerably more than doubled between 1933 and 1937 and was continuing to rise. What was at issue was whether, in the circumstances of 1937, further expansion of public sector invest-ment was a condition of maintaining expansion. It is immediate or postponed public investment with which he was concerned; the experience of the 1930s had shown the practical difficulties of quickly expanding it and there were fears that the expected end of the housing boom in 1937 might require it in 1938.

What can and what cannot be inferred from this in more general terms about Keynes and his general approach to such problems? If it is being argued that Keynes was not an expansionist *à l'outrance*, whatever the circumstances and whatever the implications, I myself believe that to be true. One has not only this evidence but also the evidence of wartime. But if it is being argued that he had ceased by 1937 to regard as near an approach as was possible to full employment as the right longer-term objective, I believe that to be nonsense and there is lots of post-1937 evidence to prove that. Keynes did not cease to think about peace-time during the war years. I cannot claim to know (and I do not think Professor Hutchison has any claim to know) exactly what his personal 'trade-off' would have been between high employment, inflation and curtailment of economic liberties. If he was doubtful about the practicability of Beveridge's 3 per cent of unemployment, my own belief is that his doubts had nothing directly to do with effects on inflation; they were primarily concerned with structural change and structural unemployment and with difficulties of making very high employment consistent with a balance of payments. I doubt, that is to say, whether Keynes was a Pseudo-Keynesian, if by that is meant exclusive concern with certain limited aspects of macro-economics and complete oblivion of the micro-economic aspects of continuing change and adjustment. I doubt equally whether

Keynes's human values were those of some of the more extreme 'liberal' economists of today and I doubt their right to appropriate the title of the only true disciples of the author of 'The End of Laissez Faire'.

June 1977   AUSTIN ROBINSON

Rejoinder

by

T. W. HUTCHISON

1. It is very surprising that Lord Kahn should begin by resorting to Sir Dennis Robertson's remark about a 'composite Aunt Sally of uncertain age'. For Robertson used this phrase for the purpose of denouncing comprehensively the Keynesian concept of 'classical' economics. This concept involves extensive generalisations – partly justified, partly not – about almost two centuries of economic theorising. On the other hand, the adjective 'Pseudo-Keynesian', in respect of its composition, or fount and origin, can be very specifically defined and limited in terms, primarily, of three well-known authorities, but for whom the phenomenon could hardly have come into existence. They are Lord Kahn, Joan Robinson and Sir Roy Harrod, although, of course, their enormous influence and prestige brought them numerous followers, allies, partners, popularisers and subsidiaries. Nor is there any question of 'uncertain age': precise dates are given for all quotations and precise birthdays are available in *Who's Who*. Though the three prime Pseudo-Keynesians differ, of course, on a number of issues, they share a very great deal of common ground; *and especially, all three have been repeatedly, for decades, concerned to invoke, quite unjustifiably, the magic, charismatic name of Keynes on behalf of their own particular policy doctrines.* Anyhow, while on the subject of composite Aunt Sallies, Lord Kahn should turn his attention to his colleague Joan Robinson's concept of 'Bastard Keynesians' (which would seem, almost inevitably, to include Keynes himself).

2. General complaints about 'tracking down quotations' and 'lifting out of context' may often be taken to indicate a desire to ward off criticism or keep the record under cover. For *any* critical examination of *any* record *must* require 'tracking down quotations'; and one cannot quote, at less than virtually infinite length, without, *to some extent*, lifting passages 'out of context'. *Of course* quotations, like statistics, or any other kind of empirical evidence, can, inten-

tionally or unintentionally, be misrepresentative or misleading. If this is the case with any of my quotations, let it be shown. But certainly attempts to set out the record will appear obnoxious, and even subversive of well-established attitudes, to those able or eager to maintain complacency about the recent history of economics and economic policy in Britain.

3. Lord Kahn states that

> 'there seems to be no justification for Professor Hutchison's statement that "in 1937 Keynes was clearly concerned with the possible dangers of inflation when unemployment was still around 11 to 12 per cent".'[1]

But the undeniable facts are (1) that the unemployment percentage in January–March 1937 *was* around 11 to 12 per cent; and (2) that Keynes *then* observed that the economy might be 'approaching rather near the limit' regarding inflation, *and called for cutting back public expenditure.* Keynes certainly did *not* argue in January–March 1937: 'If and when unemployment falls to 6–7 per cent *at that point* cuts should be made'. He called for cuts *then and there*, and for 'a different technique' for reducing unemployment than that of 'a further general stimulus at the centre'. It is rather disturbing to find Lord Kahn protesting that there is 'no justification' for the historical facts being what they undeniably are. Of course I do *not* maintain that Keynes regarded 12 per cent as the minimum to be aimed at, nor that this was the natural rate at the time; and, in any case, Lord Kahn's estimate of 6–7 per cent is more than enough amply to justify the contrast I am concerned with in respect of subsequent Pseudo-Keynesian doctrines, as expounded by himself, Joan Robinson and Sir Roy Harrod.

4. Lord Kahn alleges that I am 'unaware of the terrible controversy which was raging in the second half of the 'thirties about the pace of rearmament'.[2] But regarding this 'terrible controversy' – unforgettable by anyone who lived through those years – Lord Kahn fails to produce *any* evidence or references whatsoever to show that it had *any* relevance for Keynes's views on employment targets in peace-time. As already noted, Professor Moggridge, the

---

[1] Above, p. 49.

[2] Above, p. 49.

authority on the Keynes papers, recently maintained[1] that he had 'not as yet come across sufficient evidence' to support the 'construction' placed by Lord Kahn on Keynes's articles of 1937 – a construction in some ways highly discreditable to Keynes. In his Comment *Lord Kahn has still failed to produce any relevant evidence.* Moreover, it is quite irrelevant that Keynes was stressing 'radically different' viewpoints on policy in 1939-40 from those he had put forward in 1937. The whole situation and prospects regarding peace and war had radically changed between the two dates.

5. Whether or not my statements about the natural rate of unemployment are 'foolish', I am quite content to leave to any of the numerous distinguished economists around the world who understand and use this concept.[2] It should be noted, however, that Lord Kahn suggests that it is 'foolish' *even to use such a concept, or talk about the natural rate, at all.* This suggestion seems to be the latest example of a kind of terminological or conceptual dogmatism which seeks to ban the use of particular words or concepts – as in the past such terms as 'hoarding' and 'forced saving'. The late Professor H. G. Johnson related discerning and amusing reminiscences of this dialectical tactic in his paper 'Cambridge in the 1950s'.[3]

6. Lord Kahn devotes more than half of his Comment to the defence of his views on policy. This is understandable, though these views, over the years and decades, have been constantly stated and restated – and as often answered, most recently by Mr Eltis:

'A notable feature of recent economic history is that the successful economies have not in general been those with a detailed network of government regulations and controls over wages, prices, trade and investment. On the contrary, they have been economies which have given the price mechanism great scope to allocate resources. It is therefore puzzling why so many Keynesians wish to run the British economy in an essentially East-European or at any rate Crippsian way.'[4]

---

[1] *Keynes,* 1976, p. 177.

[2] 'Keynes's idea of the level of unemployment which would exist without demand deficiency seems astonishingly similar to Milton Friedman's "natural" rate of unemployment.' (S. Brittan, in G. D. N. Worswick (ed.), *The Concept and Measurement of Involuntary Unemployment,* 1976, p. 259.)

[3] *On Economics and Society,* University of Chicago Press, 1975, pp. 107 ff.

[4] Walter Eltis, 'The Keynesian Conventional Wisdom', *Lloyds Bank Review,* July 1977, p. 38.

But surely what is *really* 'puzzling' is not that some economists want to run the economy in an East European way, but that these economists should be called (or permitted to call themselves) 'Keynesians'. But all this is totally irrelevant to the central theme of my *Paper,* which is about the history of economic doctrines. Regarding Lord Kahn's views on economic policy, past and present, *the one single point I am concerned to establish is that in respect of several of his most important views, e.g. relating to targets for unemployment and price stability, there is no justification at all for regarding them as Keynesian or neo-Keynesian, or for assuming that Keynes would have approved of them rather than that he would have described them, in his famous phrase, as 'modernist stuff gone wrong and turned sour and silly'.*

7. Regarding Sir Austin Robinson's contribution: it should be noted that it offers no support at all to Lord Kahn's explanation in terms of rearmament. Indeed, Sir Austin maintains that in 1937 Keynes was concerned about the balance of payments and 'a rising marginal import-ratio'.[1] On the contrary, Keynes stated (*The Times,* 13 January, 1937) exactly the opposite:

> '. . . it is now advisable . . . to welcome imports even though they result in an adverse balance of trade . . . above all, it is desirable that we should view with equanimity and without anxiety the prospective worsening of our trade balance . . .'[2]

However, it is easy to agree with Sir Austin that Keynes's primary concern was with 'structural' factors. The profound and perennial structural rigidities of the British economy have been, and are, a main determinant of the natural rate of unemployment, or of the level of employment which can be maintained without danger of inflation.

---

[1] Above, p. 58.

[2] Reproduced in Appendix A, p. 70.

J. M. Keynes after 'The General Theory . . .'

APPENDIX A

*How To Avoid A Slump**

I. THE PROBLEM OF THE STEADY LEVEL

It is clear that by painful degrees we have climbed out of the slump. It is also clear that we are well advanced on the upward slopes of prosperity – I will not say 'of the boom', for 'boom' is an opprobrious term, and what we are enjoying is desirable. But many are already preoccupied with what is to come. It is widely agreed that it is more important to avoid a descent into another slump than to stimulate (subject to an important qualification to be mentioned below) a still greater activity than we have. This means that all of us – politicians, bankers, industrialists, and economists – are faced with a scientific problem which we have never tried to solve before.

I emphasise that point. Not only have we never solved it; we have never tried to. Not once. The booms and slumps of the past have been neither courted nor contrived against. The action of Central Banks has been hitherto an almost automatic response to the unforeseen and undesigned impact of outside events. But this time it is different. We have entirely freed ourselves – this applies to every party and every quarter – from the philosophy of the *laissez-faire* state. We have new means at our disposal which we intend to use. Perhaps we know more. But chiefly it is a general conviction that the stability of our institutions absolutely requires a resolute attempt to apply what perhaps we know to preventing the recurrence of another steep descent. I should like to try, therefore, to reduce a complicated problem to its essential elements.

The distressed areas

It is natural to interject that it is premature to abate our efforts to increase employment so long as the figures of unemployment remain so large. In a sense this must be true. But I believe that we are approaching, or have reached, the point where there is not much advantage in applying a further general stimulus at the centre. So long as surplus resources were widely diffused between industries and localities it was no great matter at what point in the economic structure the impulse of an increased demand was applied. But the evidence grows that – for several reasons into which there is no space to enter here – the economic structure is unfortunately rigid,

---

*The three articles by Keynes under this general heading were published in *The Times* on consecutive days, 12, 13, 14 January, 1937.

and that (for example) building activity in the home counties is less effective than one might have hoped in decreasing unemployment in the distressed areas. It follows that the later stages of recovery require a different technique. To remedy the condition of the distressed areas, *ad hoc* measures are necessary. The Jarrow marchers were, so to speak, theoretically correct. The Government have been wrong in their reluctance to accept the strenuous *ad hoc* measures recommended by those in close touch with the problem. Nevertheless a change of policy in the right direction seems to be imminent. We are in more need today of a rightly distributed demand than of a greater aggregate demand; and the Treasury would be entitled to economise elsewhere to compensate for the cost of special assistance to the distressed areas. If our responsibility in this direction could be thus disposed of we could concentrate with a clear mind on our central problem of how to maintain a fairly steady level of sustained prosperity.

Why is it that good times have been so intermittent? The explanation is not difficult. The public, especially when they are prosperous, do not spend the whole of their incomes on current consumption. It follows that the productive activities, from which their incomes are derived, must not be devoted to preparing for consumption in any greater proportion than that in which the corresponding incomes will be spent on consumption; since, if they are, the resulting goods cannot be sold at a profit and production will have to be curtailed. If when incomes are at a given level the public consume, let us say, nine-tenths of their incomes, the productive efforts devoted to consumption goods cannot be more than nine times the efforts devoted to investment, if the results are to be sold without loss. Thus it is an indispensable condition of a stable increase in incomes that the production of investment goods (which must be interpreted in a wide sense so as to include working capital; and also relief works and armaments if they are paid for by borrowing) should advance *pari passu* and in the right proportion. Otherwise the proportion of income spent on consumption will be less than the proportion of income earned by producing consumption goods, which means that the receipts of the producers of consumption goods will be less than their costs, so that business losses and a curtailment of output will ensue.

Difficulty of 'planning'

Now there are several reasons why the production of investment goods tends to fluctuate widely, and it is these fluctuations which cause the fluctuations, first of profits, then of general business activity, and hence of national and world prosperity. The sustained enjoyment of prosperity requires as its condition that as near as possible the right proportion of the national resources, neither too much nor too little, should be devoted to active investment (interpreted, as I have indicated, in a wide sense). The proportion will be just right if it is the same as the proportion of their incomes which the community is disposed to save when the national resources of equipment and labour are being fully employed.

There is no reason to suppose that there is 'an invisible hand', an automatic control in the economic system which ensures of itself that the amount of active investment shall be continuously of the right proportion. Yet it is also very difficult to ensure it by our own design, by what is now called 'planning'. The best we can hope to achieve is to use those kinds of investment which it is relatively easy to plan as a make-weight, bringing them in so as to preserve as much stability of aggregate investment as we can manage at the right and appropriate level. Three years ago it was important to use public policy to increase investment. It may soon be equally important to retard certain types of investment, so as to keep our most easily available ammunition in hand for when it is more required.

The longer the recovery has lasted, the more difficult does it become to maintain the stability of new investment. Some of the investment which properly occurs during a recovery is, in the nature of things, non-recurrent; for example, the increase in working capital as output increases and the provision of additional equipment to keep pace with the improvement in consumption. Another part becomes less easy to sustain, not because saturation point has been reached, but because with each increase in our stock of wealth the profit to be expected from a further increase declines. And, thirdly, the abnormal profits obtainable, during a too rapid recovery of demand, from equipment which is temporarily in short supply is likely to lead to exaggerated expectations from certain types of new investment, the disappointment of which will bring a subsequent reaction. Experience shows that this is sure to occur if aggregate investment is allowed to rise for a time above the normal proper proportion. We can also add that the rise in Stock Exchange values consequent on the recovery usually leads to a certain amount of expenditure paid for, not out of current income, but out of Stock Exchange profits, which will cease when values cease to rise further. It is evident, therefore, what a ticklish business it is to maintain stability. We have to be preparing the way for an increase in sound investments of the second type which have not yet reached saturation point, to take the place in due course of the investment of the first type which is necessarily non-recurrent, while at the same time avoiding a temporary overlap of investments of the first and second types liable to increase aggregate investment to an excessive figure, which by inflating profits will induce unsound investment of the third type based on mistaken expectations.

Having made these general observations, let us examine the opportunities for putting them into practice.

II. 'DEAR' MONEY
THE RIGHT TIME FOR AUSTERITY

In one respect we are better placed than ever before. On previous occasions a shortage of cash has nearly always played a significant part in turning the boom into the slump. Prices and wages are sure to rise somewhat with an increase in output. Nor is there anything wrong in that; for it is to be sharply distinguished from the so-called 'vicious spiral' which attended the post-War currency inflations. But the higher incomes resulting from increased output at a higher level of costs naturally require more cash. Formerly there was seldom a sufficient margin of cash which could be made available to finance the higher incomes. Thus the resulting shortage of cash led to a rise in the rate of interest, which, developing at a time when the maintenance of investment was already becoming difficult for other reasons, had a fatal influence on confidence and credit, and decisively established the slump.

But this time there is no risk of a cash shortage in those countries which still maintain a free economic system and are enjoying a normal recovery. The currency devaluations, the huge output of gold, and the newly-won elasticity of the foreign exchanges have combined to give us the needed freedom of action. We no longer rest under a compulsion to do what is ruinous. Unfortunately there is a widely held belief that dear money is a 'natural' consequence of recovery, and is, in such circumstances, a 'healthy' feature.

Playing with fire
Unquestionably in past experience dear money has accompanied recovery; and has also heralded a slump. If we play with dear money on the ground that it is 'healthy' or 'natural', then, I have no doubt, the inevitable slump will ensue. We must avoid it, therefore, as we would hell-fire. It is true that there is a phase in every recovery when we need to go slow with postponable investment of the recurrent type, lest, in conjunction with the non-recurrent investment which necessarily attends a recovery, it raises aggregate investment too high. But we must find other means of achieving this than a higher rate of interest. For if we allow the rate of interest to be affected, we cannot easily reverse the trend. A low enough long-term rate of interest cannot be achieved if we allow it to be believed that better terms will be obtainable from time to time by those who keep their resources liquid. The long-term rate of interest must be kept *continuously* as near as possible to what we believe to be the long-term optimum. It is not suitable to be used as a short-period weapon.

Moreover, when the recovery is reaching its peak of activity, the phase of non-recurrent investment in increased working capital and the like will be almost over; and we can be practically certain that within a few weeks or months we shall require a lower rate of interest to stimulate increased investment of the recurrent type to fill the gap. Thus it is a fatal mistake to use a high rate of interest as a means of damping down the boom. It has been the occurrence of dear money hitherto which has joined with other forces to make a slump inevitable.

If the Stock Exchange is unduly excited or if new issues of a doubtful type are becoming too abundant, a higher rate of interest will be useless except in so far as it affects adversely the whole structure of confidence and credit. Moreover, alternative methods are available. A hint to the banks to be cautious in allowing their names to appear on prospectuses, and to the committee of the Stock Exchange to exercise discrimination in granting permissions to deal would be more efficacious. And if necessary a temporary increase of a substantial amount in the stamp on contract-notes (as distinguished from transfers) in respect of transactions in Ordinary shares would help to check an undue speculative activity.

Nevertheless a phase of the recovery may be at hand when it will be desirable to find other methods temporarily to damp down aggregate demand, with a view to stabilising subsequent activity at as high a level as possible. There are three important methods open to our authorities, all of which deserve to be considered in the immediate future.

Boom control

Just as it was advisable for the Government to incur debt during the slump, so for the same reasons it is now advisable that they should incline to the opposite policy. Aggregate demand is increased by loan-expenditure and decreased when loans are discharged out of taxation. In view of the high cost of the armaments, which we cannot postpone, it would put too much strain on our fiscal system actually to discharge debt, but the Chancellor of the Exchequer should, I suggest, meet the main part of the cost of armaments out of taxation, raising taxes and withholding all reliefs for the present as something in hand for 1938 or 1939, or whenever there are signs of recession. The boom, not the slump, is the right time for austerity at the Treasury.

Just as it was advisable for local authorities to press on with capital expenditure during the slump, so it is now advisable that they should postpone whatever new enterprises can reasonably be held back. I do not mean that they should abandon their plans of improvement. On the contrary, they should have them fully matured, available for quick release at the right moment. But the boom, not the slump, is the right time for procrastination at the Ministry of Health.

Just as it was advisable (from our own point of view) to check imports and to take measures to improve the balance of trade during the slump, so it is now advisable to shift in the opposite direction and to welcome imports even though they result in an adverse balance of trade. I should like to see a temporary rebate on tariffs wherever this could be done without throwing British resources out of employment. But, above all, it is desirable that we should view with equanimity and without anxiety the prospective worsening of our trade balance which is likely to result from higher prices for raw materials and from our armament expenditure and general trade activity, even though this may put a temporary strain on the Exchange Equalisation Fund. The recent decrease in the Bank of England's fiduciary issue indicates that we have today a plethora of gold. It is desirable, therefore, that the raw material countries should be allowed to replenish their gold and sterling resources by sending their goods to us; especially so in view of the difficulties which would remain in the way of foreign lending on the old scale even if the existing artificial obstacles were to be removed. This policy is doubly desirable. First, because it will help to relieve a temporarily inflated demand in the home market. But, secondly, because a policy of allowing these countries to increase their resources in 1937 provides the best prospect of their using these resources to buy our goods and help our export industries at a later date when an increased demand in our home market is just what we shall be wanting.

These, I urge, are the methods which will best serve to protect us from the excesses of the boom and, at the same time, put us in good trim to ward off the cumulative dangers of the slump when the reaction comes, as come it surely will. But we also need more positive measures to maintain a decent level of continuous prosperity. In a third article we will conclude with suggestions to this end.

III. OPPORTUNITIES OF POLICY
A BOARD OF PUBLIC INVESTMENT?

While we shall be prudent to take such steps as I have indicated to prevent the present recovery from developing into a precarious boom, I admit that I do not see much sign of this, except, perhaps, in certain special directions. For the moment we have the rearmament expenditure superimposed on the building activity and on the large non-recurrent investment in working capital and in renewals which are characteristic of a recovery as such; and that is a situation which suggests caution.

But, on the other hand, our export industries remain, on the whole, inactive; the peak of the non-recurrent investment in increased working capital (which in the last two or three years has been much larger per annum than the cost of rearmament now is) may be behind us; sooner or later the building activity will relax: and the cost of rearmament is neither permanent nor large enough while it lasts to sustain prosperity by itself (in 1936 at least seven or eight times as much was spent on new building as on rearmament). Thus our main preoccupation should be concerned not so much with avoiding the perils of a somewhat hypothetical boom as with advance precautions against that sagging away of activity which, if it is allowed to cumulate after the usual fashion, will once again develop into a slump. Too much alarm about a hypothetical boom will be just the way to make a slump inevitable. There is nothing wrong with the very moderate prosperity we now enjoy. Our object must be to stabilise it and to distribute it more widely, not to diminish it.

Positive precautions

Thus we need constructive preparations against the future. Recent experience has shown us how long it takes to prepare for useful investment; and what careful handling is necessary to develop a psychological state in the investment market which will accept a reduction in the long-term rate of interest. Moreover, it will be much easier to check a recession if we intervene at its earliest stages. For, if it is allowed to develop, cumulative forces of decline will be set in motion which it may prove almost impossible to check until they have run their course. If we are to be successful we must intervene with moderate measures of expansion before the decline has become visible to the general public. One factor only shall we have in our favour – namely, the improvement in our export trade with the raw-material countries which I now anticipate with confidence at a date not far distant. In other directions we shall be hard put to it, in my opinion, to develop useful activities on an adequate scale. The menace of the next slump, and what that would mean to our institutions and traditions, if it comes, should be at our elbow, urging us to new policies and boldness of mind.

Perhaps it is absurd to expect Englishmen to think things out beforehand. But if it is not, there are various thoughts to think. So far I have stressed the importance of investment. But the maintenance of prosperity and of a stable economic life only depends on increased investment if we take as unalterable the existing distribution of purchasing power and the willingness of those who enjoy purchasing power to use it for consumption. The wealthier we get and the smaller, therefore, the profit to be gained from adding to our capital-goods, the more it is incumbent on us to see that those who would benefit from increasing their consumption – which is, after all, the sole ultimate object of economic effort – have the power and the opportunity to do so. Up to a point individual saving can allow an advantageous way of postponing consumption. But beyond that point it is for the community as a whole both an absurdity and a disaster. The natural evolution should be towards a decent level of consumption for every one; and, when that is high enough, towards the occupation of our energies in the non-economic interests of our lives. Thus we need to be slowly reconstructing our social system with these ends in view. This is a large matter, not to be embarked upon here. But, in particular and in detail, the relief of taxation, when the time comes for that, will do most for the general welfare if it is so directed as to increase the purchasing power of those who have most need to consume more.

Planning investment

The capital requirements of home industry and manufacture cannot possibly absorb more than a fraction of what this country, with its present social structure and distribution of wealth, chooses to save in years of general prosperity; while the amount of our net foreign investment is limited by our exports and our trade balance. Building and transport and public utilities, which can use large amounts of capital, lie half-way between private and public control. They need, therefore, the combined stimulus of public policy and a low rate of interest. But a wise public policy to promote investment needs, as I have said, long preparation. Now is the time to appoint a board of public investment to prepare sound schemes against the time that they are needed. If we wait until the crisis is upon us we shall, of course, be too late. We ought to set up immediately an authority whose business it is not to launch anything at present, but to make sure that detailed plans are prepared. The railway companies, the port and river authorities, the water, gas, and electricity undertakings, the building contractors, the local authorities, above all, perhaps, the London County Council and the other great Corporations with congested population, should be asked to investigate what projects could be usefully undertaken if capital were available at certain rates of interest – $3\frac{1}{2}$ per cent, 3 per cent, $2\frac{1}{2}$ per cent, 2 per cent. The question of the general advisability of the schemes and their order of preference should be examined next. What is required at once are acts of constructive imagination by our administrators, engineers, and architects, to be followed by financial criticism, sifting, and more detailed designing; so that some large and useful projects, at least, can be launched at a few months' notice.

There can be no justification for a rate of interest which impedes an adequate flow of new projects at a time when the national resources for production are not fully employed. The rate of interest must be reduced to the figure that the new projects can afford. In special cases subsidies may be justified: but in general it is the long-term rate of interest which should come down to the figure which the marginal project can earn. We have the power to achieve this. The Bank of England and the Treasury had a great success at the time of the conversion of the War Loan. But it is possible that they still underrate the extent of their powers. With the existing control over the exchanges which has revolutionised the technical position, and with the vast resources at the disposal of the authorities through the Bank of England, the Exchange Equalisation Fund, and other funds under the control of the Treasury, it lies within their power, by the exercise of the moderation, the gradualness, and the discreet handling of the market of which they have shown themselves to be masters, to make the long-term rate of interest what they choose within reason. If we know what rate of interest is required to make profitable a flow of new projects at the proper pace, we have the power to make that rate prevail in the market. A low rate of interest can only be harmful and liable to cause an inflation if it is so low as to stimulate a flow of new projects more than enough to absorb our available resources.

Is there the slightest chance of a constructive or a forethoughtful policy in contemporary England? Is it conceivable that the Government should do anything in time? Why shouldn't they?

APPENDIX B

*Borrowing for Defence**
Is It Inflation?

A PLEA FOR ORGANISED POLICY

The Chancellor of the Exchequer having published his prospective borrowing plans for rearmament, the question properly arises whether this programme can be superimposed on the present business situation without risking a state of inflation. The question is hotly debated. The Chancellor declares that a loan of £80,000,000 a year is not excessive in the circumstances. His critics dispute this conclusion. Clearly it is a matter of figures. The Chancellor would agree that £200,000,000 a year would be dangerous; his critics are disposed to accept £40,000,000 a year as safe. What calculations are relevant to the answer? I believe that we can carry the argument a stage further than mere assertions based on vague individual judgements.

To begin with, what do we mean by 'inflation'? If we mean by the term a state of affairs which is dangerous and ought to be avoided – and, since the term carries to most people an opprobrious implication, this is the convenient usage – then we must not mean by it merely that prices and wages are rising. For a rising tendency of prices and wages inevitably, and for obvious reasons, accompanies any revival of activity. An improvement in demand tends to carry with it an increase in output and employment and, at the same time, a rise in prices and wages. It is when increased demand is no longer capable of materially raising output and employment and mainly spends itself in raising prices that it is properly called inflation. When this point is reached, the new demand merely competes with the existing demand for the use of resources which are already employed to the utmost.

Surplus capacity

The question is, therefore, whether we have enough surplus capacity to meet the increase in demand likely to arise out of an expenditure of £80,000,000 raised by loans and not by diverting incomes through taxation. Now the resulting increase in demand will be greater than £80,000,000; since we have to provide for increased expenditure by the recipients of the £80,000,000, and for further similar reactions. There are reasons, too, detailed to repeat here, for supposing that the total effect on demand will,

---

*This article by Keynes was published in *The Times* on 11 March, 1937.

in existing conditions in this country, probably lie between two and three times the primary increase. To be on the safe side, let us take three times as our preliminary estimate, which means that the total increase in the national income resulting from the Chancellor's borrowing will have to be in the neighbourhood of £240,000,000 at present prices – an increase, that is to say, of about 5½ per cent. Have we sufficient surplus capacity to provide such an increase? Or will the Government demand merely serve to raise prices until resources, already in use, are diverted from their present employment? This is certainly not a question to be answered lightly.

The number of insured persons who are still unemployed is, indeed, as high as 12½ per cent. But though the new demand will be widely spread (since it will not be limited to the primary employment for armaments, but will also spread to the secondary employments to meet the increased demand of consumers), we cannot safely regard even half of these unemployed insured persons as being available to satisfy home demand. For we have to subtract the unemployables, those seasonally unemployed, &c., and those who cannot readily be employed except in producing for export. Unless we make a liberal allowance for overtime and more output from those already in employment, it would need more planning and transfer of labour than is practicable in the time to increase the national output in 1937 by 5½ per cent over what it was in 1936; although over (say) a period of three years it might be possible.

Thus it is not plain sailing. If we suppose the full rate of Government spending to begin immediately, without any improvement in the export industries or any reduction in other activities, unsupported by organised overtime, by careful planning and an interval for the planning to take effect, there is a risk of what might fairly be called inflation. Is the Chancellor's claim that he can avoid inflation nevertheless justified? For the following reasons I believe that it is.

Other resources

In the first place, my 'multiplier' of three times may, in present circumstances, exaggerate the scale of the repercussions. As prosperity increases, saving probably increases more than in proportion; particularly when profits are rising. It may well be that the total increase in expenditure, resulting from loans of £80,000,000, will be no more than (say) £170,000,000, or 4 per cent of the national income – an improvement which it would be much easier to accomplish than 5½ per cent.

In the second place, some part of the new demand will be met, not by increasing home output, but by imports (which I have not allowed for in the above calculation). This means either that the imports will be offset by increased exports or, failing this, that there will be a diminution of net foreign investment. Probably there will be a bit of both. We can look forward to an increase of 'invisible' exports through the increased earnings of our shipping and our foreign investments and, perhaps, from visitors to the Coronation. But it remains particularly advisable to do anything possible to stimulate our staple exports. For it is there that our reserves of surplus labour are chiefly to be found. It is no paradox to say that the best way of avoiding inflationary results from the Chancellor's loan is to increase both imports and exports. In any case, we can make a deduction of (say) 15 to 20 per cent on account of increased imports, which brings down the increase in the national output (apart from exports) necessary to avoid inflation to a figure between $3\frac{1}{2}$ and $4\frac{1}{2}$ per cent.

Thirdly, measures to ensure that all possible orders are placed in the Special Areas where surplus resources are available will greatly help. It is a mistake to suppose that this is merely a form of charity to a distressed part of the country. On the contrary, it is in the general interest. Whether demand is or is not inflationary depends on whether it is directed towards trades and localities which have no surplus capacity. To organise output in the Special Areas is a means of obtaining rearmament without inflation. I am not sure that this is properly understood. One feels that the War Departments are inclined to regard a Special Areas measure as a form of charity, doubtless praiseworthy, which interferes, however, with their getting on with the job in the most efficient way. On the contrary, it is only by using resources which are now unemployed that the job can be got on with, except at the cost of great waste and disturbance. The Special Areas represent our main reserve of resources available for rearmament without undue interference with the normal course of trade. They are not a charity, but an opportunity.

We are still assuming that new capital investment, apart from rearmament, will continue on the same scale as before. It seems possible, however, that there will be some reduction in new building. By an extraordinary and most blameworthy short-sightedness, our authorities do not think it worth while to collect complete statistics of new building, the figures for the County of London being omitted from the published aggregate. But new building may easily fall short of last year by £20,000,000, which would provide a quarter of the Chancellor's requirements. There remains capital development carried out by the railways, public boards, and local authorities, which should be to some extent controllable by deliberate policy. On the other hand, increased investment may be necessary in some directions, to provide new plant where marked deficiencies exist. Nevertheless a net increase in output of 3 per cent might see us through, after allowing for the other offsets we have mentioned: and that is an improvement we might reasonably hope to accomplish in the near future.

Need for planning
I conclude that the Chancellor's loan expenditure *need* not be inflationary. But unless care is taken, it may be rather near the limit. This is particularly so in the near future. It is in the next year or eighteen months that congestion is most likely to occur. For ordinary investment is still proceeding under the impetus of the recent years of recovery. In two years time, or less, rearmament loans may be positively helpful in warding off a depression. On the other hand, the War Departments may not succeed – they seldom do – in spending up to their time-table.

This conclusion is subject, however, to an important qualification. The Government programme will not be carried out with due rapidity, and inflation will not be avoided, by happy-go-lucky methods. The national resources will be strained by what is now proposed. It is most important that we should avoid war-time controls, rationing and the like. But we may get into a frightful muddle if the War Departments merely plunge ahead with their orders, taking no thought for general considerations affecting foreign trade, the Special Areas, and competing forms of investment.

I reiterate, therefore, and with increased emphasis the recommendation with which I concluded my former articles in *The Times*. It is essential to set up at the centre an organisation which has the duty to think about these things, to collect information and to advise as to policy. Such a suggestion is, I know, unpopular. There is nothing a Government hates more than to be well-informed: for it makes the process of arriving at decisions much more complicated and difficult. But, at this juncture, it is a sacrifice which in the public interest they ought to make. It is easy to employ 80 to 90 per cent of the national resources without taking much thought as to how to fit things in. For there is a margin to play with, almost all round. But to employ 95 to 100 per cent of the national resources is a different task altogether. It cannot be done without care and management; and the attempt to do so might lead to an inflation, only avoidable if a recession happens to be impending in other directions. The importance of collecting more facts deserves particular attention. For my estimates, given above, are of course no better than bold guesses based on such figures as are accessible. They are obviously subject to a wide margin of error.

Index of Authors

Index of Subjects

Keynes versus the 'Keynesians' ...?

PRESS COMMENTS on the First Edition

'Professor T. W. Hutchison reviews, with a wealth of quotations and comment, the relevance of Keynes' writings to the present times as distinct from the 1930s. He argues that some economists, who have claimed for their particular policy proposals that they reflected Keynesian theories, have no foundation for such claims.'

Accountant

'Professor Terence Hutchison argues that on several crucial issues Lord Keynes would be nearer to the so-called monetarist economists of today than to those labelled Keynesian.'

The Times

'Ever since the war, the predominant school of economists in this country has been labelling itself Keynesian after Lord Keynes, whose new and rather magical economic policies they were (they said) advocating. And since what they advocated involved high state spending to cure unemployment and promote economic growth . . . it was not surprising that the new school of thought was enthusiastically supported by the Socialists. But was Keynes himself really a Keynesian? This intriguing question is discussed in *Keynes versus the 'Keynesians' ...?*

Yorkshire Post, in an Editorial

'The study is timely ... Now that the "gang of four" (Robinson, Kaldor, Harrod, Kahn) has been refuted, we are left ruefully asking why it should have taken 30 hard years. The answer may be that we are no wiser than our forebears. But from Adam Smith till the 'twenties there was a learning process; the past 50 years seem to have entailed unlearning what had been learned in Georgian and Victorian days. In part, this may be nemesis for the hubris which turned Victorian and Edwardian into pejoratives. In part, it is the result of seeking short cuts to Utopia. We must make our way back from these blind alleys as best we can, grateful to the IEA for a sceptic's eye view of the maze.'

Daily Telegraph, in an Editorial

HOBART PAPERBACKS in print

1. POLITICALLY IMPOSSIBLE . . . ?   W H HUTT
1971   75p
'Hutt feels that economists have deserted their intellectual integrity in commenting on current economic affairs by advancing judgements conditioned by what they believed would be well received by the political group in power.'
John Biffen, MP—*The Spectator*

2. GOVERNMENT AND THE MARKET ECONOMY   SAMUEL BRITTAN
1971   75p
' . . . makes out a case for a modern version of the market economy that is at once sensible and stimulating . . . '   Rt Hon Harold Lever, MP—*Financial Times*

3. ROME OR BRUSSELS . . . ?   W R LEWIS
1971   75p
' . . . suggests that the choice for the future in the Market is between reinforcing individual economic freedoms and "a new European-scale version" of existing bureaucratic over-centralised Governments.'
Leader—*Daily Telegraph*

4. A TIGER BY THE TAIL   F A HAYEK
Compiled and introduced by SUDHA R SHENOY
1972   Second Edition 1978   £1·50
'. . . incredibly apposite . . .'   Leader—*Daily Telegraph*

5. BUREAUCRACY: SERVANT OR MASTER?   WILLIAM A NISKANEN
with Commentaries by:
DOUGLAS HOUGHTON, MAURICE KOGAN, NICHOLAS RIDLEY and IAN SENIOR
1973   £1.00
'Niskanen argues, with some cogency, that every kind of pressure on a bureau head leads him to maximise his budget.'   Peter Wilsher—*Sunday Times*

6. THE CAMBRIDGE REVOLUTION: SUCCESS OR FAILURE?   MARK BLAUG
1974   Revised Edition 1975   £1.50
'The controversy is over the theories of growth, capital and the determination of income distribution.'   Ian Steedman—*The Times Higher Education Supplement*

8. THE THEORY OF COLLECTIVE BARGAINING 1930-1975   W H HUTT
with Commentaries by LORD FEATHER and SIR LEONARD NEAL
1975   Second Impression 1977   £2·00
'. . . a powerfully-argued economic case . . .'   *Liverpool Daily Post*

9. THE VOTE MOTIVE   GORDON TULLOCK
with a British Commentary by MORRIS PERLMAN
1976   £1.50
'It's an entertaining and illuminating thesis.'   *Sunday Times*

10. NOT FROM BENEVOLENCE . . .   RALPH HARRIS/ARTHUR SELDON
1977   Second Impression 1977   £2·00
'If one is to hazard a guess about which organisation has had the greatest influence on public economic understanding, it would [be] the Institute of Economic Affairs.'   Samuel Brittan—*Financial Times*

Extracts from

Keynes versus the 'Keynesians' . . . ?

PROFESSOR HUTCHISON:

1. 'With the benefit of hindsight, inadequacies and dangers can certainly be discerned in Keynes's doctrines (as, indeed, they were at the time by Pigou, Robertson and Henderson).'

2. 'A more cautious and modest view on the part of his followers of the gains achieved by the Keynesian "revolution" . . . might have been in order.'

3. '. . . the most serious weakness was political: that is, an over optimism, perhaps even naïveté, regarding the possibility o enlightened management of the economy by popularly-elected governments.'

4. '. . . it is quite unjustifiable to proclaim as "Keynesian", or "neo Keynesian", views which conflict seriously with those which Keynes expressed in some of his last relevant pronouncements.'

5. '. . . it is certainly unjustifiable to imply that the views on employ ment targets and policies which came to be described a "Keynesian", in the 1950s and 1960s, were those held by Keynes or that they would have been approved by Keynes had he lived.

6. '. . . Keynes did not regard it as necessary or desirable to rel primarily or predominantly on government controls, which mus be used, as he put it, "not to defeat but to implement the wisdon of Adam Smith".'

7. 'Keynes certainly did not show himself in the least optimistic o complacent about the effectiveness of government controls ove trade or wages, regarding which Pseudo-Keynesians were to b so persistently over-optimistic in the ensuing decades.'

8. '. . . while the Master's magic name was frequently invoked o behalf of the new conventional unwisdom [on expanding aggre gate demand to reduce unemployment, economic growth, th higher importance of full employment over price stability incomes policies to counter inflation, and the sanctity of publi expenditure], *it is impossible to find statements of these new doctrines in Keynes's writings*.'

LORD KAHN

9. 'In a letter [by Keynes] . . . in December 1943 . . . can be seen th germs – but no more than the germs – of incomes policy, unde which the rate of increase in wages and prices is largely deter mined as a result of negotiations on a political plane.'

SIR AUSTIN ROBINSON:

10. 'I doubt . . . whether Keynes was a Pseudo-Keynesian, if by that i meant exclusive concern with certain limited aspects of macro economics and complete oblivion of the micro-economic aspect of continuing change and adjustment. I doubt equally whethe Keynes's human values were those of some of the more extrem "liberal" economists of today . . .'

ISBN 0-255 36101-7   *Second Impression*   £2·0

THE INSTITUTE OF ECONOMIC AFFAIRS
2 Lord North Street, Westminster,
London SW1P 3LB   Telephone: 01-799 374